THE URBAN CHURCH IMAGINED

The Urban Church Imagined

Religion, Race, and Authenticity in the City

Jessica M. Barron and Rhys H. Williams

NEW YORK UNIVERSITY PRESS

New York

NEW YORK UNIVERSITY PRESS
New York
www.nyupress.org

References to Internet websites (URLs) were accurate at the time of writing. Neither the author nor New York University Press is responsible for URLs that may have expired or changed since the manuscript was prepared.

Library of Congress Cataloging-in-Publication Data
Names: Barron, Jessica M., author.
Title: The urban church imagined : religion, race, and authenticity in the city /
Jessica M. Barron and Rhys H. Williams.
Description: New York : NYU Press, 2017. | Includes bibliographical references and index.
Identifiers: LCCN 2017008080| ISBN 9781479877669 (cl : alk. paper) |
ISBN 9781479887101 (pb : alk. paper)
Subjects: LCSH: City churches.
Classification: LCC BV637 .B28 2017 | DDC 253.09173/2—dc23
LC record available at https://lccn.loc.gov/2017008080

New York University Press books are printed on acid-free paper, and their binding materials are chosen for strength and durability. We strive to use environmentally responsible suppliers and materials to the greatest extent possible in publishing our books.

Manufactured in the United States of America

10 9 8 7 6 5 4 3 2 1

Also available as an ebook

CONTENTS

ACKNOWLEDGMENTS

Scholarship is never developed alone. We would like to take this opportunity to thank those who so generously gave of their time and assistance in seeing this project through from initial idea to finished book. That starts with Japonica Brown-Saracino, who provided a tremendous amount of support, feedback, direction, advice, and encouragement throughout the data collection and first drafts of this project. Thank you to Jane Sell and Rogelio Saenz for acting as excellent sounding boards throughout the process. Your mentorship and guidance were invaluable. A special thanks to our colleagues Gwendolyn Purifoye, Reuben Miller, Ryon Cobb, Louwanda Evans, and Collin Mueller for your tireless dedication to seeing this project through to publication. Thank you for all of your theoretical insights, careful and hopeful critiques of previous drafts, and above all, your emotional support.

We want to thank the Department of Sociology and affiliates of the McNamara Center for the Social Study of Religion at Loyola University of Chicago. Specifically, this includes Courtney Ann Irby and Todd Nicholas Fuist for engaging in countless hours of stimulating conversations that helped to better frame ideas, assisting with chapter edits, and sharing always helpful comments at presentations. Many thanks to the Department of Sociology and Race and Ethnic Studies Institute at Texas A&M University for providing intellectual and financial support that allowed completion of the research and help in the writing. We thank both departments for providing the type of intellectual space where we were never short of encouragement or support to complete the book. Lori Couch and Jesús Gregorio Smith were of immense help as they assisted in transcribing hours of interview files and also shared their invaluable insights.

We are happy to work with New York University Press. Thank you to our editor, Jennifer Hammer, for her editorial acumen and good suggestions; you were dedicated to the development of the work while supporting our scholarly independence. Thanks also to Amy Klopfenstein for her expert care of the manuscript. Our thanks to the anonymous reviewers who first read the book proposal and sample chapters and then the final manuscript; we appreciate your time and valuable feedback. Session audiences and fellow participants at the meetings of the Society for the Scientific Study of Religion, the Association of Black Sociologists, the American Sociological Association, and the Southwest Sociological Association asked questions, offered praise and critique, and ultimately supported our conviction that we had something here. The collegial nature of these organizations, in our experiences, prompted conversations and ideas that served the further advancement of the project. Parts of chapters 3 and 4 appeared in Jessica M. Barron, "Managed Diversity: Race, Place, and an Urban Church," *Sociology of Religion* 2016 (77:18–36), and are reprinted with permission.

To the people of Downtown Church, we extend our gratitude and thanks. We are especially grateful to the members of Downtown Church who gave freely of their time, knowledge, and sacred lives. Thank you to all who opened up their homes and sanctuaries, to those who allowed Jessica to ride with you on the train, to join in on your dinner plans, and just become a part of your world. We learned so much from your insights, responses, and dedication.

Finally, to our families. To the Barron and Villa families from Jessica—thank you for your unwavering support and constant nurturing of my ideas. You gave me the freedom to ask the hard questions and the space to work through the answers. To Kelly from Rhys—thank you for always talking over ideas and always sharpening my thinking. I know I am a better sociologist, and I hope a better person, because of you.

Introduction

Race, Church, City

Crystal was a transplant to Chicago. She had been in the city a few years, chasing a creative career in music and art. She was a fair-skinned black woman with a large auburn afro and a warm smile. She was one of the first people I [Barron] met when I moved to Chicago to pursue a graduate degree. During one of our many excursions together, Crystal turned to me, visibly excited for what she was about to share. She said, "You should come to this place I found. It is kind of like this weird church but there are a lot of hot black guys there." Her excitement grew as she attempted to describe this peculiar place that she hesitated to call a church. Her excitement was convincing and a few days later we hopped on a bus at 5 p.m., headed downtown. We got off a few blocks from the downtown core and walked toward a large brick building. There were a few office buildings and specialty boutiques surrounding our final destination, which turned out to be a performing arts theater. The air was crisp and the wind mild but steady. It was on the warmer side of days in late September Chicago. The smell of something spicy and tangy filled the air. It was coming from an upscale Thai food restaurant across the street, with a valet parking line that reached the length of the street.

Once we turned the corner toward the front entrance of the theater, we saw two very large banners with the church's signature logo, which mimics the Major League Baseball logo, and large letters that read "Welcome to Downtown Church." The banners stood upright about 8 feet. They were positioned in front of a cement staircase that led to the deep-set entrance to the building. As we entered, a very attractive black man and a white woman greeted us. They were stylish in their dress, greeting us with bright white smiles, eager to open the doors. Then we moved into a darkened theater lobby. The ticket counter was to my left, where a theater employee was still selling tickets for a show that would premier the next day. The room was filled with young, attractive, well-dressed, racially diverse women and men. They all seemed to be laughing, hugging, and catching up on the week's events. I couldn't help but think that on first impression it felt closer to a singles mixer or "meet-up" group for young professionals than a church service. On the left side of the main entrance there were three sets of double doors, all red, and closed. Red velvet ropes, reminiscent of those used at a Hollywood premier night, guarded them. On this night, the doors were also guarded by a 23-year-old, six-foot-three-inch-tall black man. He reminded me of a bouncer at a club; he was nicely dressed, guarding the door until the service was about to begin. In his hand he held the weekly bulletins, which he handed to attendees when the doors opened. Upon entering through the double doors we were met with live music from the worship band. The red theater seats stood out through 20 rows of stadium seating. There was a large screen above the stage and two portable screens on each side displaying the church logo. At the top of the middle section there was a large sound booth where two men sat and controlled the lights and the screens.

The service began. The band was live, loud, and upbeat, just like a pop concert. The worship band was a group of young, black, Asian, and white singers and musicians. There was a row of singers in front. Behind them were an electric guitarist, bassist, drummer, an acoustic guitarist, and a keyboardist. The music section of the worship service lasted for 22 minutes, which was almost half of the service. As the pacing and emotion of the songs built, the lights and sound adjusted accordingly; lights got brighter or dimmer as the music got softer or louder. Everyone in the congregation was standing during the entire worship set. Many were singing along with the words displayed on all three screens. Some were bobbing their heads, others had their hands up; some were doing a small dance at their seat. A couple of girls were screaming. And another group of congregants had their phones in the air, waving them around as if they were front row at a concert. One of the women sitting next to me was visiting the church for the first time. She leaned over and said, "I know this is church but I just can't help shaking my ass to this song." After the worship set was over, Pastor Phil walked to the center of the stage, and stood at a clear podium that held a sleek MacBook laptop. He is tall, about six-feet-four-inches, has a warm round face and strategically messy blonde hair. He wore a fitted black, button-down shirt with an embellished print across the entire shirt. He had on designer jeans and black leather shoes with a square toe. He began to deliver his message, reading from his laptop. He was shy in his delivery, making little eye contact, and stumbling through the first few points of his sermon. He wasn't the charismatic speaker generally associated with evangelical pastors, nor did he seem to fit with the glitz and glam of the congregation. He had a much more reserved presentation. However, congregants didn't seem to mind. Some of them clapped or shouted an encouraging "Amen" after he completed a point. Others nodded while looking up scriptures or apps on their phones. The sermon was short and ended a bit abruptly. The lights brightened, the band came back out to sing an "exit" song, and folks began to congregate, chat, and walk to the exit. I am sure that Crystal saw the perplexed look on my face and pulled me in, saying, "see I told you, this place is strange, huh?" She began to chuckle and said, "I see the wheels in your head churning and I can literally hear your mind clicking away!" She was right. I immediately put on my "sociology hat" and began plotting a way to study what seemed to be an unconventional congregation—one that was joining a new wave of churches using unconventional spaces in city centers to appeal to young people across the country.

This book tells the story of one religious congregation that self-consciously uses "the city" and aspects of its historical and current imagery as the basis for establishing itself and attracting members. "Downtown Church," as we call it, is a "planted" congregation, an outreach effort by a mega-church that exists well outside the metropolitan area to which it orients itself. The "home" church is non-denominational evangelical Protestant, and exists and flourishes in the context of the deep history of innovative evangelical organizational efforts to confront and convert worldly society. Downtown Church, as its extension, exists at the intersection of two distinct orientations of white evangelical Protestantism directed toward urban America. One is a deep suspicion and even fear of cities as sites of sin, social problems, and societal decay. The other is a calling to use the tools of an energetic faith to evangelize the city. Downtown Church also exists within—and in part reacts to—the deeply racialized character of American society and culture, which has its own conceptualization of the urban and all that it means.

Downtown Church aims to appeal to a particular image of the city in order to find a niche in its competitive metropolitan religious market, as well as use that image to establish a marker of collective identity that engages its target constituency—the young, upwardly mobile, and hip. In its advertisements, self-presentations during worship services and other activities, and in consistent remarks made by the pastoral leadership, Downtown Church portrays "the city" as a site of trendy excitement—a place for sophisticated, enthusiastic, and fashionable people. Consumption of material goods is assumed to be a sign of this urban trendiness, such as pricey clothing or the latest technology. Another central element assumed to represent the urban scene and its culture is "diversity." Diversity is understood as "natural," even definitional, to "the city." Varieties of social backgrounds, skin colors, and aesthetic tastes mark the urban as a potpourri of cultural diversity. To be truly of and in the city, according to the guiding vision of Downtown Church, it must be a place in which diversity flourishes for all to consume.

And yet, in implementing this vision, tensions—even contradictions—abound. The church leadership studiously avoids racialized cultural expressions of worship even as it celebrates itself for not being "too white." The congregation revels in its central city location, even as the pastoral leadership continues to live in exurban Indiana near the home church and must commute in each weekend. The fashionably clad bodies of black members are given volunteer positions that highlight their visibility and silently scream for attention to their presence, even as the actual leadership staff remains all white. And in outreach efforts designed to put the church on the map within the community, the church consistently trips over its painfully obvious lack of familiarity with Chicago politics. In its quest to fulfill its pastoral charge of becoming a "challenging, relevant and never boring"[1] church for Chicago's young urbanites, Downtown Church is met with the complexities of the racial legacy embedded in Chicago's urban landscape, alongside the city's current status as a post-industrial global city. As members, leaders, and volunteers take part in the development and production of this congregation, their different and sometimes contradictory ideas of the city are brought to the forefront.

This book examines the ways in which race, class, gender, and consumption intersect with spatial context to shape the racialized experiences of members of this diverse religious organization. It argues that the urban environment fosters a particular expectation of racial diversity, what we call a "racialized urban imaginary." This imaginary is often not articulated directly, but its existence as a part of Downtown Church's worldview exposes the "utility" of race, that is, the usefulness of using race—and literally the bodies of persons of color—as a way to foster a particular identity for the church, which in turn legitimates the organization in its new and unfamiliar environment. Church leaders and congregants negotiate between their imagined ideas of what a church in the city should look like and the structures of inclusion and exclusion these imaginaries help to create and recreate.

Diversity and the City

"The City" has been a contested space in American history and culture. It has been contested as a social space in which many diverse groups live in physical proximity and must negotiate a coexistence. It has also been a symbolically contested space in which the *meaning* of the city has been disputed, celebrated, and condemned. As Orsi (1999) has observed, since the beginning of the transition from an agrarian to an industrial society, the city has often been used to represent in the popular imagination a contrast to that which is "truly America"—while native-born America is conceived as white, cities are multi-hued and immigrant. While America is Protestant, cities are Catholic, Jewish, Muslim, or secular. While America is temperate, cities are the sites of vice.

It has not been a coincidence that the growth of American cities has often corresponded with the influx of large numbers of immigrants. Industrialization and urbanization produced job opportunities, and large numbers of Europeans, Latin Americans, Asians, and others came to the United States to fill the ranks of factory workers in the mid- to late nineteenth century and in the early twentieth century. Significantly, many newcomers were Catholic and Jewish, and were darker-skinned (Williams 2016). It is not an exaggeration to say that cities became the place where America met the world, and many scholars have examined that multifaceted encounter (e.g., Higham 1955; Gusfield 1963; Schrag 2010). Of course, not all immigrants became city dwellers, as many saw an unsettled country as a huge draw. The United States' westward ex-

pansion was built on exploring the frontier and searching for new land
and a place to settle and build a home. But the expanding cities of the
East Coast and northern industrial belt heralded a new America, and
offered a direct challenge to those national stories that saw the nation as
a place set apart, a New World that left the Old World and its social ills
behind. Cities became seen as threats to the purity and homogeneity of
small-town America, particularly in the cultural imagery of the Midwest
(see Williams 2004). The proverbial "all-American boy/girl" was, and
remains, white, blond, Protestant, and small-town.

Despite—and indeed, because of—the cultural mythologies of urban
spaces as corrupt, fallen, and potentially dangerous, American Protestantism has also viewed cities as mission fields. While the homogenous
small town may be an image that aligns well with the quintessential
Protestant form of religious organization—the local congregation—
attempts to convert and reform the city have been consistent in American evangelical history. Famous preachers such as Charles Grandison
Finney and Dwight Moody brought their messages and their revivalist
styles specifically to urban spaces, determined to save them (McLoughlin 1980). What is sometimes termed the "third Great Awakening" had
an urban dimension at its very center. At the same time, the "Social Gospel" movement was also often centered in cities, such as Jane Addams's
Hull House in Chicago, in what was then a progressive attempt to "solve"
the problems brought on by immigration, industrialization, and expanding metropolises (Luker 1998). Less concerned with salvation than with
social reform, Social Gospel proponents nonetheless saw the emerging
urban landscape as the place where Christians were most needed. Thus,
while American Protestantism in many ways is rooted in the cultural
story of white, rural, and small-town life, by the twentieth century it was
also working diligently to make itself "at home in the city" (Lewis 1992).[2]

More recently, the city has been a social and cultural beacon, a place
to make or re-make one's life and living, beyond just a place where there
are jobs. The city has become a symbol of the energy and progress that is
a major theme in the American story. It is a place where opportunity and
freedom await, where entrepreneurial activity produces our proud economic affluence, where human-built national icons such as the Empire
State Building have announced our place on the world stage. The city is
a place where there is cultural richness, excitement, and adventure, and

where the diversity that we have claimed to value in America is most on display.

Thus, the cultural "imaginary" of the city in American life is complex, multifaceted, and occasionally contradictory. It produces allure and revulsion, with unintended and contradictory effects on social and cultural dynamics. However, it is not static. Diversity has long been understood as a defining feature of modern society (Simmel 1971). But by the 1980s, the embrace of neoliberal urban development strategies by city governments resulted in a consumer-based posture toward diversity. As Zukin (1995) and Grazian (2004, 2007) have shown, the "urban experience" has become a commodity for consumption; the affluent and educated middle class has come to expect to consume diversity as part of the city experience (see, for example, Hummon 1990). Such expectations of diversity align easily with an internationalist and individualist vision that sees racial and ethnic differences as exotic, aesthetically pleasing, and simultaneously slightly dangerous but controlled. It is not unlikely, then, that congregations moving into metropolitan areas would engage in a form of cultural production that makes use of urban symbols of consumption. Downtown Church, in its explicit orientation to this ethos, may be more unusual.

Any discussion of race and urbanicity within the United States is a discussion of racial inequality and segregation of black Americans, who remain at the bottom rungs of the socioeconomic ladder (Massey and Denton 1993). Throughout US history, economic, social, and political transitions have been guided by oppressive legal and ideological traditions which have resulted in the entrenchment and persistence of black disadvantage (Wilson 1996). Within the context of space, these patterns have resulted in black Americans being disproportionately concentrated in urban locations, making urban ghettos synonymous with the black community (Massey and Denton 1993; Wacquant 2001).

In much of mainstream discourse, "urban" has become a euphemism for "black" in describing neighborhoods, cultural styles of music and dress, and social problems such as gangs or drugs (Johnson 2003). The perpetuation of this linkage can be referred to as *racialization*, a process of ascribing racial or ethnic identities to a relationship, social practice, location, or group that did not identify itself as such (Omi and Winant 1994). Racialization is often born out of a power struggle where one group ascribes an identity to the other for the purpose of continued domination. Similarly, *racial formation*, a concept also popularized by Omi and Winant (1994), is described as "a process occurring through a linkage between structure and representation . . . a racial project is simultaneously an interpretation, representation, or explanation of racial dynamics, and an effort to reorganize and redistribute resources along particular racial lines" (56). Consequently, racialized images and history connect with a consumerist approach to engaging the city.

"Urban" is also an adjective that calls up images of young people, cutting-edge style, and progressive cultural politics—instantiated in such phrases as "Young Urban Professionals" or in brandings such as "Urban Outfitters." Urban congregations capitalize on "black as urban" as well as "young urban professional" in their pursuit of diversity. Diversity thus becomes an interactive process, engaging race in both direct and non-racial ways (Berrey 2005).

Race and White Evangelical Protestantism

Just as the encounter with the city has been ambivalent for white evangelical Protestantism, so has been its encounter with race, racial segregation, and racial inequality in the United States. At a very basic level, it is not unfair to observe that the most solidly evangelical region of the country is also the region that was most marked by slavery, had a legal racial apartheid system, and continues to be most conservative on issues of race and racial equality. Emerson and Smith (2000) and Wadsworth (2014), among others, show convincingly the ways in which evangelicalism has supported, either directly or indirectly, racial segregation and inequality.

On the other hand, some white evangelicals have tackled directly the problem of racism in American society and their own responsibility for it. Some of this effort has been connected to the missionary impulse to evangelize all peoples, but there have also been concerted efforts toward what is often called "racial reconciliation" (Emerson and Smith 2000).

One result of these efforts is called the Evangelical Racial Change Movement (ERCM). The marquee goal is to have, where feasible, churches that seek to create racially and ethnically diverse, culturally syncretic congregations, wherein no single ethnic group or worship style dominates (Emerson and Woo 2006; Wadsworth 2014). At the beginning of the twenty-first century, the messages of racial diversity and racial reconciliation were increasingly overlapping among white evangelicals, resulting in an effort by many Christians to worship in racially diverse congregations—a similar push for diversity as that seen in secular organizations around that same time. As a result, multiracial congregations in urban areas have become a growing organizational trend among evangelicals.

Religious congregations are one of the most pervasive public gathering places in American society. Chaves (2004:1) noted, "no voluntary or cultural institution in American society gathers more people more regularly than religious congregations." Yet, like many institutions in this country, congregations are faced with the rapidly changing racial demographics of the United States and they struggle to integrate their organizations (Emerson and Woo 2006). Christian-based congregations, in particular, garner much attention from scholars as organizations that largely remain racially segregated despite sincere efforts to fulfill their moral ethos of come one, come all (DeYoung et al. 2003).

Multiracial congregations are notable, even if not common, as racial diversity is quite rare in most social institutions in the United States. Multiracial congregations have been covered not only in evangelical media outlets such as *Christianity Today*, but in the likes of *TIME* magazine, the *Huffington Post*, and E! network's short-lived reality show, "Rich in Faith." As a result, some scholars, evangelical leaders and intellectuals, and many clergy are eager to understand how religious racial diversity could contribute to challenging or even dismantling systems of social stratification (Cobb, Perry, and Dougherty 2015; Christerson and Emerson 2003). Multiracial congregations also offer insights into organizational structures that create race-centered initiatives of incorporation and keep discussion of racial difference at the forefront of their motivations for integration (Collins 2011).

In *Ambivalent Miracles*, Wadsworth (2014) meticulously traces the rise and evolution of the ERCM (1990–2010) that spearheaded the corporate charge to worship in racially diverse congregations. The ERCM transitioned to promote what evangelicals called the Multiethnic Church Movement (MEC). For ERCM advocates, multi-ethnic congregations are the pinnacle of reconciliation efforts (Emerson and Woo 2006). The

ERCM and MEC spawned a lively debate on the role of race in diverse religious organizations either as a salient feature that inevitably produces congregational division (Edwards 2008) or as a status attendees transcend in multi-ethnic settings to achieve a collective identity as believers (Marti 2008). Multiracial congregations are often defined as: (1) a congregation where no one racial group is 80% or more of the membership; or (2) a congregation in which there is a likelihood that two randomly selected people in the congregation will belong to different racial groups (Emerson and Woo 2006; Dougherty and Huyser 2008). A recent report by the 2010 Faith Communities Survey found that 14% of US congregations are multiracial. While this number seems small, the increase in interracial marriages, the sizable growth among immigrant and multiracial populations, and the overall increase of populations of color within the last three decades (Lee and Bean 2007) will more than likely contribute to the proliferation of multiracial congregations across the nation. Because the previously mentioned study shows that a growing percentage of minorities are attending religious services in multiracial congregations, many of which are newly established, a comprehensive understanding of the association between congregational characteristics and race-related outcomes must give attention to these emerging congregations.

Sociological research on multiracial and multi-ethnic congregations has examined the dynamics that keep Christian congregations in the United States largely racially segregated (e.g., Edwards 2008; Emerson and Yancey 2008; Marti 2008). A number of important insights have been generated by this work—arguably the most significant is the importance of organizational intentionality. The dynamics uncovered help to shed light on the efficacy in confronting race and racial privilege for congregations that want to integrate (Emerson and Woo 2006). Drawing from organizational sociology and the sociology of race and ethnicity, the research has two main premises. First, the organizational characteristics have an impact on individual-level outcomes for those involved, including beliefs and attitudes, and organizational diversity (or for Blau 1977, "differentiation") can have adverse effects on the attitudes and experiences of the organization's members (Christerson, Edwards, and Emerson 2005; Emerson and Woo 2006; Martinez and Dougherty 2013). Second, that race is central to the organization of society and its institutions, and multiracial congregations generally need to placate white members, and affirm their religio-cultural preferences and interests, in order to sustain their participation (Edwards 2008). This argument suggests that multiracial congregations remain racialized, and will, in most cases, reaffirm rather than challenge racial norms in America.

However, despite growing attention to the role of organizational characteristics in shaping the beliefs, identities, behaviors, and experiences of multiracial church attendees, there are some limitations in that literature. First, the majority of these studies in this area view racial processes as more or less self-standing, devoid of any mention of gender and economic class (Yancey and Kim 2008). In contrast, works by "intersectionality" scholars show that a myriad of statuses and identities, particularly those based on race, class, and gender, combine to shape the life experiences of groups (Collins 1999; Crenshaw 1993; Read and Eagle 2011). Persons have multiple identities, different ones of which may be salient in different social settings or actions. In turn, these multiple identities affect how they are perceived and treated by other people and within social institutions. Second, and most important, many studies of multiracial congregations tend to focus on successful and large multiracial congregations in cities in which measures of residential segregation are lower than the national average. Thus, there is a certain amount of "sampling on the dependent variable" involved—which leads to uncertainty regarding whether the dynamics of such congregations are the same when the congregations are new, are small, or are in different geographical settings. Exploring these trends within a city that has a special history with residential segregation is particularly imperative.

Religious Congregations and the City

The *Baylor Institute for Studies of Religion* reported in 2008 that recent organizational trends have resulted in an increased percentage of Christian-based congregations moving into downtown metropolitan areas in order to sustain organizational growth—downtown areas that are of course in the processes of urbanization, gentrification, increasing diversity, and continuing racial residential segregation. The increase in diversity in such cities is notable. Whereas the proportion of non-white groups in US metropolitan areas stood at 16.6% in 1980, by 2010 the proportion had risen to 28.6% (Lee, Iceland, and Sharp 2012). This trend was particularly pronounced in cities such as New York, Los Angeles, Houston, and Chicago.

Many Mainline Protestant churches have been grappling with the demographic changes of city centers for years (e.g., Form and Dubrow 2005). They have had to adjust programming, welcome new social groups into the congregation, and negotiate with downtown businesses and commercial interests in order to maintain their impressive—but aging—church buildings. As Ammerman (1997) and others have shown, some have managed these changes more successfully than others, and one of the challenges they face are newly planted evangelical congregations.

The spatial shifts among evangelical congregations, which are included in this increasing presence in cities, are slowly but noticeably bucking the tide of "white flight" out of urban areas. These shifts engender questions about how traditionally homogeneous organizations make demographic transitions. How do they become inclusive? Do the experiences of varied racial groups within a church differ when a congregation exists in a more diverse spatial context? How might a different racial context affect organizations that have historically been (and in many cases still remain) racially segregated? The dynamics of religion, race, and the city have received substantial research attention in recent years (e.g., Marti 2008; McRoberts 2003; Patillo-McCoy 1999), but despite these studies, the organizational practices through which predominately white religious organizations interact with new, racially diverse environments as they develop a new organizational identity remain unclear.

The move of new populations back into downtown areas—whether gentrifying yuppies or new empty-nesters wanting more neighborhood amenities and less house-and-yard maintenance—has also resulted in part in a mainstream merging of commercial and religious culture. Increasing numbers of congregations are trying to provide a place for congregants to reconcile the traditional tensions between "holiness" and the broader consumer culture. Downtown Church is an excellent example of this effort—it wants to use the city to establish a niche in a competitive metropolitan religious setting, as well as using the image of "the city" as a marker of collective identity that speaks to the young, hip, "unchurched" urban dweller. The church meets in the rented theater building in the city's downtown, holding services on Sunday evenings, and self-consciously uses the location to proclaim itself as different, authentic, and urban.

The notion of "city-life" is embedded in the church's experience of place and the built environment, its boundaries, expectations, inclusions, and fabrications. Part of the city's allure is its cultural location, as a place where the middle class (who increasingly have trouble affording to live in the affluent parts of major cities) can consume diversity—as experience, as entertainment, and as a part of personal identity (Lloyd 2006; Mele 2000). However, their expectations of dress, speech, consumption, and racial interaction can serve as reminders of the rigidity of the color line and enact a static notion of the city. It is at this intersection of consumption, place, and identity that this book explores what we will call the *racialized urban imaginary* of Downtown Church and the structures of inclusion and exclusion that they help to create and recreate.

Authenticity and the Imaginary

This book refers to the "imagined" city for two reasons. The first is inductive from the research itself. In the overwhelming majority of interviews and throughout our ethnographic work, we found Downtown Church congregants and leaders continually using the term "imagine" to make a distinction between the ways in which the suburban-based leadership team and city-based congregants envisioned "their city." Often there was a connotation of criticism in the use of the term—congregants from Chicago thought the leadership "imagined" the city to be different from what it was in reality. Sometimes the connotation of "imagine" was more like "imagination," reflecting the idea that something new or innovative was developing. In either case, and for both church leaders and members, they were talking, planning, and acting within the context of an "imaginary"—a set of cultural ideas and images that form a mental picture. This book's goal is not to prove which imagination is "correct" or, in cases of disagreement, which opinion is more valid. Instead, its aim is to discuss how these varied and oftentimes dueling imaginations rely on racialized, classed, and place-based understandings of the city of Chicago and of its urban residents.

In Benedict Anderson's famous work *Imagined Communities* (1991), he described the idea of the nation imagined. He argued that if one feels oneself to be a member of a nation, one feels a certain kinship or con- nection to people one has never and will never meet; in part, one must imagine that connection rather than experience it directly. The nation is a fraternity of "limited imaginings" made up of "horizontal comrade- ship" and culturally significant systems tied to what is imagined. Con- ceptually, this framing of imagined communities describes, to a certain extent, the dynamic of the imagined city for Downtown Church. As they seek to develop the identity of a church *in* the city of Chicago and *for* the city of Chicago, congregants and leaders wrestle not only with their conception of the city but also with each other's imagined city. Further- more, these congregants and leaders rely on each other logistically to sustain the church and to creatively grow the church into their ideal congregation.

Second, the idea of the "imagined city" guides our discussion of "au- thenticity." Leaders of Downtown Church are eager to create an authen- tic urban establishment in order to attract authentic urban members. Thus, we conceptualize authenticity as a cultured understanding of what is real and true, in contrast to what is faked, put on, or superficial. Au- thenticity is informed by a collective imagination; it is itself not objec- tive but simply a more-or-less shared set of beliefs about the nature of things we value in the world because they can be relied upon to be "real." Authenticity is reinforced by the conscious efforts of cultural produc- ers and consumers alike. David Grazian (2004) notes that authenticity shares two related aspects, one of which will be used throughout our analysis, "it can refer to the ability of a place or event to conform to an idealized representation of reality; that is, to set expectations regarding how such a thing ought to look, sound and feel" (10). Authenticity is alluring to outsiders due to its status as something that is not readily accessible to the mainstream public—in a sense, a privileged mystique. However, the search for authenticity as true and not consciously created will always be a failing prospect as authenticity is always manufactured (Grazian 2004; Peterson 1997). Moreover, the search for authenticity presumes a static existence rather than a complex and contradictory one. Thus, in the quest for authenticity, we tend to rely on stereotypes, often frozen from a particular point in time, as a guide (Grazian 2004; Johnson 2003). Richard Peterson (1997) claims that authenticity is not inherent in an object or event that is designated to be authentic, but rather is a socially agreed-upon construct. Thus, authenticity is ironically always fabricated.

Similarly, Grazian (2004) suggests there is a sliding scale of authenticity and thus almost anything can be regarded as more or less authentic in relation to its competitors. The sliding scale allows tailoring of collective memory and fabrication of authenticity to serve the needs of the present. As a result, the business of authenticity can be a lucrative market (Grazian 2004; Peterson 1997). Capturing authenticity through fabrication to meet culturally shaped expectations is a common strategy by producers in cultural industries such as film, television, music, or art.

Authenticity can also be a place-based concept as place is equally valuable for cultural production. The allure of standing on the exact same location as Emily Dickinson, Martin Luther King, Jr., or C. S. Lewis helps to drive tourist industries around the world. Discussions of authenticity are often dependent upon a shared understanding of a particular place or location (Grazian 2004; Lloyd 2006; Peterson 1997). Downtown Church uses the expectations of urban space to set the expectations for how their church should look, sound, and feel. However, neither leaders nor members are positioned to claim authentic Chicago fully, simply because it does not exist as an unchanging entity.

An Ethnographic Exploration

This book employs an ethnographic approach to explore the cultural contours of Downtown Church, its orientations to congregational diversity, how it shapes its actual organizational practices, and how that dynamic illuminates broader currents in American religious culture as religious organizations grapple with how to engage with and become a part of urban environments across the nation. The volume draws on a systematic analysis of race-related and consumer-oriented discourse in 55 semi-structured and ethnographic interviews, and content analysis of sermons, marketing materials, and web content, combined with 18 months of fieldwork. In all aspects of this work we were dedicated to understanding the attendant fears, goals, and organizational practices surrounding the presence of certain minority groups within the congregation, and to investigating these orientations and practices as having gendered and classed dimensions as well as racial ones.

First author Barron collected all the empirical data and conducted all interviews.[3] As a racially ambiguous, single woman of color, working with a predominantly white, male leadership staff, her presence generated insightful exchanges. Barron was repeatedly questioned about her racial identity by the pastoral staff, who often had difficulty placing her ethno-racially. She was often approached by the pastoral staff regarding her "unique look" and engaged in discussions about how her racial ambiguity could help pastors traverse racial boundaries within the congregation. Pastors rarely asked her directly to racially identify, but would ask her, for example, "What are black people saying [or what are the Latino members saying] in your interviews?"

Barron's racial identity wasn't the only topic of discussion. The pastoral staff had many concerns surrounding her "singleness" as it pertained to interviewing their male congregants and leaders. She had to convince the leadership staff that she was a trained social scientist and that interviewing is part of a scientific method—not a way to pick up single men at the church. In many ways, her status as a graduate student provided her with the authority, class rank, and respect that her gender did not. However, as other women who engage in ethnographic methods have experienced, some congregants took her offer for an interview as an open invitation for a date. Barron routinely maneuvered through these gendered and raced interactions from the "outsider within" perspective (Lorde 1984:114; Collins 1999), offering a distinct lens through which to explore the intersection of race, class, and gender within the congregation.

This book examines various components of Downtown Church including its history, organizational structure, programming and marketing materials, outreach endeavors, rituals, and worship services. We engaged in participant observation of evening worship services and other church-related activities such as dinners, leadership meetings, and community-building events. Field notes were taken during all services and church-related activities. All field notes were recorded on pads of paper during the services. Note-taking during the worship service is common in evangelical congregations, as congregants regularly bring Bibles and take notes on the pastor's lesson; thus, this activity did not disturb congregants as they worshipped. However, during other church-related activities, notes were jotted on napkins and on a smart phone.

These notes were then coded based on recurring themes centered on references to the city, racial and gendered patterns in group dynamics, interracial interactions, references to/use of technology, use of popular culture and consumption in sermons, and congregational changes over time.

Thirty-five ethnographic interviews and 20 semi-structured interviews were conducted. These interviews were transcribed and coded with the aid of two assistants. Ethnographic interviews differ from semi-structured ones in that the former are usually conducted in the field and not at a separate location. There is not a written set of questions and a particular order in which they are asked. Ethnographic interviews are sometimes referred to as unstructured interviews (Bell 1995; Whyte 1993). They are interviews conducted in the field to uncover new topics of interest; gain understandings of meanings behind a specific event, ritual, or practice; or to capture reactions and responses to an event (e.g., a sermon, outreach event, women's group) in that moment (Burawoy 1998). Although many of these interviews appear to be simple conversations, both parties were aware that it was an informal interview process. Additionally, in the beginning of fieldwork, ethnographic interviews are especially useful for getting the lay of the land and gaining trust among the people involved in the social settings being examined (Feldman, Bell, and Berger 2003; Brown-Saracino, Fine, and Thurk 2008). The ethnographic interviews lasted anywhere from 15 minutes to two hours, and were conducted with 15 men and 20 women, ranging in ages from 19 to 47.

The semi-structured interviews were a convenience sample. Barron conducted all of the semi-structured interviews after one year of being in the field. The formal interviewing was delayed so that Barron could develop relationships and generate a consistent and visible presence in the church. There is an intimate quality to sacred spaces, and relationships in congregations can be quite intense and meaningful for church members. Barron handed out flyers before and after worship services at the information tables and around the theater lobby, outlining the study and need for participants. Interview criteria were women and men, 18 years of age and over who had attended the church consistently for at least three months. These interviews were recorded on a digital recorder. Interviews were conducted in offices, coffee shops, restaurants, and in some cases, the home of the participant.

Ten women and ten men, who ranged in age from 22 to 42 years and ranged in racial and ethnic background, participated in formal interviews. Participants also ranged in their levels of church involvement. However, 60% of those interviewed were in some leadership or volunteer position during their time at the church. This significant engagement was due in part to the church being fairly new and relatively small. Many people who attended became involved in volunteer work at one time in their membership just to help the church get up and running. Pseudonyms are used for all participants (they chose their own pseudonyms) and for places within Chicago. The name of the church has also been changed.

We chose to study one evangelical congregation as the unit of analysis as religious congregations are the core organizational form of religion in the United States (Chaves 2004). The religious congregation has received an extraordinary amount of attention from sociologists interested in American religion. As the preeminent religious organizational form in the United States, we know a great deal, for example, about congregations going through transitions (e.g., R. Stephen Warner's *New Wine in Old Wineskins*), or the building of collective identity and religious belief (e.g., Nancy Ammerman's *Bible Believers*). We know about how congregations handle conflict (Penny Edgell Becker's *Congregations in Conflict*), and we have several works of great comparative scope (e.g., Nancy Ammerman's *Pillars of Faith*; Mark Chaves's *Congregations in America*). We have excellent work on congregations dealing with racial marginalization (Lincoln and Mamiya's *The Black Church in the African American Experience*), cultural alienation (Gerardo Marti, *Hollywood Faith*), or as sites of immigrant adaptation (e.g., R. Stephen Warner and Judith Wittner's *Gatherings in Diaspora*). Although such ethnographic study does not allow for generalizable "findings," it is invaluable for understanding the intricate details of group culture, identity formation, and how individuals and organizations construct their social worlds in a given context (Edwards 2008; Burawoy 1998). Downtown Church is a site that allows for a particularly in-depth examination of the relationships between race and place. Its self-consciousness about being in "the city" brings to the surface both explicit and implicit understandings of race, religion, and urban society. Downtown Church thinks that it needs racial diversity in order to appear to be "authentic" and representative of the city, and it promotes this "authenticity" in ways that reflect its assumptions about race, as evident in its advertising campaigns and in its use of members of color in the congregation in highly visible volunteer positions. But in their effort to draw in religious consumers, church leaders are offering a religious space that reproduces social inequality.

This work contributes to the growing collection of studies on urban religious organizations and multiracial churches, as well as emerging scholarship on intersectionality and congregational characteristics in American religious life. It fills a gap in the research on race and religion by extending the focus to the racialization and consumption of place and its effects on religious establishments. By turning the lens of critical studies of race upon religious spaces, this book illuminates the dynamic relationship between racial inequality and religious identity.

What This Book Offers . . .

This book offers an examination of a conceptual framework that we call the *racialized urban imaginary*. This is a constellation of cultural images and themes that Downtown Church's leadership and many members use when thinking of themselves as building a church "of and for the city." This framework involves understandings of the city and its relationship to race, ethnicity, and consumer culture. Like all imaginaries, it informs actual behaviors and organizational planning by influencing what people think is real, and thus what can be done, as well as informing what people think is right or proper, and thus what should be done. We call it "racialized" because the urban imaginary used is deeply intertwined with perceptions and understandings about race and diversity. Thus, the racialized urban imaginary situates the relationship between race and place and acts as a motivating factor for the types of expectations leaders and members bring to the construction of their congregation. During our observations, we found that church leaders and congregants teetered between a consumption-oriented ideology of what makes a city unique and exciting, and a model of racialized authenticity that assumed that being ethno-racially diverse was constitutive of the urban. Both the consumer and the racialized orientations worked to shape how the church understood religion in the city. These orientations, however, were not an either/or set of discreet choices. They were intertwined, such that ethno-racial diversity became another aspect of the city that was to be "consumed" as a way of being authentically urban. This imaginary shows us how cultural values and religious identity are deeply embedded in the structures of race, especially when enacted in an urban location. Like many nightclubs, restaurants, and other urban establishments, Downtown Church engages in a form of racially charged production and consumption due to the racialization of the urban landscape (Grazian 2004, 2007).

This book sheds light on the nuances of the racialized urban imaginary and how it affects the religious practices, organization, and identity of this newly formed congregation. We pay specific attention to an organizational practice we have conceptualized as *managed diversity*. Managed diversity describes an approach to portraying the church's "brand"—its image—as diverse and "hip" to external audiences who might be interested in the congregation, as well as to the church members themselves as a means of self-understanding. Managed diversity reflects a series of techniques church officials engage in: (1) to appropriate elements of urban blackness both in its cultural forms and in the literal bodies of church members who are people of color; (2) to strategically manage the visibility of black volunteers; and (3) to carefully avoid racialized texts and religious practices within their congregation. The management of diversity legitimizes the congregation as not being "too white," but also tries to keep the church from being perceived as a "black church." It aims to create a public image and a self-identity as a racially diverse, authentically urban establishment appropriate for a young urban demographic.

Last, this book examines what we define as the *racial utility* of racially diverse congregants, as a tool that leaders use in managing diversity and authenticating their identity as a church for the city of Chicago. *Racial utility* occurs when the racial status of an individual serves the corporate needs of those in authority, in this case, the leadership staff at Downtown Church. In this congregation, the racial utility of members of color is incorporated to symbolize a fabricated diversity, imagined as a necessity for a church located in the city. Racial integration is done in ways that are nonthreatening to the organizational control of white leaders who in many ways are unfamiliar with the racial heterogeneity in their congregation. While the belief in the necessity of racialized bodies in an urban location is not a new concept for urban establishments (Grazian 2004; Johnson 2003), the adaptation of these methods by a religious organization is relatively new territory in the organizational survival methods of religious congregations.

These three ideas exist in something of an embedded conceptual order, with the racialized urban imaginary as a grounding (or over-arching) set of understandings and assumptions within which the congregation exists, and managed diversity as a set of techniques orga-nizational leaders employ to align their vision of the church with their understandings of "the city." Finally, racial utility emerges as a specific technique that reveals clearly the connections between race, religion, and the city.

What to Expect

Chapter 1 surveys the history of Downtown Church, its leadership struc-ture, and efforts to distinguish itself as a "downtown" church rather than an "inner-city" church. It analyzes how white church leaders, as outsid-ers from the suburbs of Indiana, came to pastor a church in an urban location. Further, it examines some of the larger cultural understand-ings of Chicago specifically. This discussion sets up a solid conceptual framework for the presentation of more "up close" fieldwork material (participant observation and interviews) from within the congregation and within its outreach endeavors. Chapter 2 focuses on the process of constructing an urban identity for Chicago's young adults. It illus-trates how the pastoral staff, as cultural producers, manufactures and promotes authenticity through gendered and class-based assumptions of the city, as becomes evident in their advertising campaigns, worship space, and sermonizing. Chapters 3–5 each address a specific group and/or organizational practice in order to advance our understanding of how Downtown Church leaders and congregants break new ground for their church while negotiating racial boundaries as they foster a distinctive organizational identity. Chapter 3 examines the pursuit of a racialized authenticity by church leaders through "managed diversity." This practice involves the explicit management of the visible presence of their black volunteers as a direct response to the structural relation-ship between black Americans and the urban environment. Chapter 4 examines the church's participation in a city-sponsored men's basketball league and as volunteers at one of the worst inner-city high schools in Chicago. As congregants and leaders get involved in outreach endeavors, it results in more substantive social contact across race, class, and in some cases, gender divides. The use of racial utility, and its intersection with the racialized urban imaginary, becomes particularly clear. Chapter 5 exposes the complexities of navigating the urban environment and its diversity through unforeseen romantic interracial interactions. The rumors and gossip surrounding interracial couples by church leaders and congregants work as boundary markers for particular types of interracial interaction deemed appropriate within this urban congregation. Chapter 6 then shows how, despite systematic forms of exclusion on the part of the leadership, a variety of outcomes emerges from the "managed diversity" framework. These include a discourse of commitment and hope among volunteer staff and members who are dedicated to a racially integrated religious experience in a racially divided city. This discourse promotes an active participant model—fueled by the frustration of living in segregated Chicago—advocated by a majority of participants that looks different from previous work on integrated congregations. The Conclusion provides a summary of the major arguments of the book, synthesizing the mechanisms through which the racialized urban imaginary informs white church leaders and diverse congregants of the practices and ideologies needed to create an unconventional religious space in an urban city.

1

City Jesus

I mean it is kind of interesting, you know? You walk in and it's like bam! All of these pretty people in all different [skin] colors wearing all these cute hip clothes, designer bags, designer shoes, designer jeans. I sometimes think the pastors are really trying to make this place seem like young and urban because they are from Indiana. It's like suburban kids playing dress-up in the city. Sometimes it's just over the top.
—Crystal, black congregant

In 2007, Downtown Church (DC) opened its doors. Pastor Phil and his wife Emily were both 26 years old at DC's founding and had two young sons at that time. They are a white, upper-middle-class family from a wealthy Indiana community within the large metropolitan orbit that surrounds Chicago. By the time the research for this book began, Downtown Church was a congregation of approximately 200 members. Although the pastor and his leadership staff are white, and most reside in the nearby Indiana region even after having founded Downtown Church, their new congregation's mission was to target nonaffiliated Chicago churchgoers. The church's purpose is to provide these city dwellers with a spiritual atmosphere that is "challenging, relevant, and never boring."

The Big Church and the Creative Team

Pastor Phil is the son of one of the Midwest's most well-known pastors, whose mega-church in northern Indiana has about thirty thousand members and averages perhaps eleven thousand in attendance on any given Sunday. With the financial backing of the mega-church, and a staff derived from his father's congregation, Pastor Phil set up Downtown Church in Chicago as a "campus" of the Indiana church. In conversations among the pastor, his staff, and congregants, Phil's father's church is often referred to as "The Big Church." The full dimensions of the involvement of the Big Church in DC's operations are unclear to many congregants, but they are fully aware that there is some relationship between the two congregations beyond the pastoral bloodline.

The Big Church is a typical example of the successful suburban mega-churches that have become common in evangelical Protestantism in America (see, for example, Ellingson 2007; Thumma and Travis 2007). Pastor Phil's parents run a large staff that manages five weekly services, countless internal ministries, large-scale worship and theatrical productions, retail stores, and an unaccredited college. There is a Starbucks in the church's physical plant. The Big Church provided a staff for Phil in order to assist the founding and early operations of the Chicago campus congregation. This group of staff members is collectively known as the *creative team* but it functions as a traditional pastoral staff. They are all men who have served in various capacities at the Big Church. The staff is responsible for developing the leadership at DC, sitting on the Elder Board, handling the budget, creating the marketing and branding campaigns for the church, and overseeing the startup of the campus. Some of the creative team members were close friends of Phil, while others were his superiors on the staff at his father's church (Pastor Phil and Emily were full-time staff at the Big Church).

Much of the marketing materials and website content for Downtown Church look identical to the materials used by the Big Church. These images mimic popular advertising campaigns used by Apple, Windows, and BlackBerry. Of course, there are some deviations in content due to the different target market and geographic location, but the packaging, labeling, logos, and overall branding remain very similar. The Big Church provides resources for all of Downtown Church's endeavors and they share the same marketing team. It is clear that the Big Church views DC as its progeny, so undoubtedly much of the overlap in promotional approach is intentional.

Yet beyond marketing materials and staff members, there are some distinct differences between the two congregations. Downtown Church goes beyond merely engaging with commercial tech culture in their advertising; images quite clearly play with themes involving flirtation, worldliness, and the type of conspicuous consumption that are often thought to mark the lifestyle of the contemporary American urban center. For example, more than one church advertisement—posted in buses and trains of the Chicago Transit Authority—is a very recognizable knockoff of a well-known liquor ad. The marketing scheme reveals that the goal is not to create a traditional family church, or to recreate the total community of the mega-church, but rather to create an innovative space that is solely directed at "the city." Indeed, Downtown Church does not necessarily see itself as a campus of the Big Church, but rather conceives of itself as a stand-alone entity, a new breed of urban church aimed at a new constituency—the young, single professional.

The conflicting identities between the home church and its plant often seep into the leadership structures of Downtown Church. Sometimes the result is an inadvertent privileging of the ideas and proposed directions that originate from the Big Church, even when the goal is to create a new kind of church. At the same time, because the Big Church is so far from Downtown Church geographically, Pastor Phil and other Chicago-based leaders have a fair amount of autonomy in how they run their organization on a day-to-day basis. The distance allows Downtown leaders to personalize their endeavors to match what they see as their target market and their new urban environment. Their conceptualizations of their location and desired congregants have become manifest through the creation and development of distinctive Downtown Church practices and branding.

Targeting the Unchurched

The creative team, along with Pastor Phil, began Downtown Church with the mission to target young adults, particularly those currently unchurched. They wanted to provide them with a spiritual atmosphere that could be integrated seamlessly into their city-based lifestyle, or at least into their image of what such a lifestyle encompasses. Pastor Phil and his staff sought to establish themselves in Chicago by attracting the young, middle-class, unchurched urbanite—an often elusive demographic with regard to church attendance. Mostly single, and racially diverse, this target group of people is perceived as enjoying high-energy worship services, marked by high-tech media, with professional productions and unorthodox sermons; in other words, a worship style perceived as less traditional—"not like church."

When we encountered Downtown Church it was a modestly sized congregation, but there was evidence that the marketing plan was effective. The congregation was mostly young adults in their twenties and thirties. There were few children or families. Downtown Church applies elements of young adult culture as a model for expanding the church and meeting the needs of its congregation—those who are delaying marriage and children, pursing advanced degrees, and starting careers. As residents of a cosmopolitan urban center, the members are people who have relatively more exposure to different cultures, races, ideologies, and religions than do most Americans (Marti 2005; Flory and Miller 2008). In Downtown Church's quest to fulfill their mission and achieve their goals, the founding leaders, the various leadership teams, and the members are confronted with differing orientations to the city of Chicago. Some members are new to the city, or even from out of state, some are long-time city residents, and some have lived much of their lives within the greater Chicagoland area but are generally unfamiliar with the city itself. All of these differing entry points to the city create varied expectations for how a church in the city should operate and who it should serve.

Evangelical Protestantism in the United States has long had a type of "entrepreneurial" organizational culture—that is, without an ecclesiastical hierarchy that governs congregational units, those who feel called are free to plant churches wherever they can, staff them as they choose, and run them as they see fit. As a result, evangelical Protestantism in the United States has often been a leader in adopting marketing strategies and new technologies—whether the revival camp meeting, or televangelism, or door-to-door marketing—to spread its messages and promote its organizations. At the same time, members themselves are free to join, and leave, whatever congregation suits them best. Thus, evangelical churches often simultaneously have very strong and authoritative pastoral leadership, and at the same time exhibit fairly democratized ideas about what the church should be and how it should be run. This paradox became evident for Downtown Church in some of the conflicting views of what Chicago is as a city and the best way to engage it. What it means to be a "city church" is not always clear or completely agreed upon.

The notion of a place-based lifestyle emerges from the vantage point of church leaders who are white, upper-middle-class and originally from an affluent, mostly white exurb in Indiana. They articulate a view of Chicago's public culture that understands city residents as young, racially diverse, middle-class, and focused on consumption. The imagery is deeply familiar to any American who regularly sees television commercials or print and media advertisements whose aim is to sell sports cars, fashionable clothing, high-end alcoholic spirits, or low-calorie beer. The creative team members who formulate the marketing schemes for Downtown Church are in a sense assuming a role as middle-class curators of the urban experience. They operate on the premise that Downtown Church's target demographic will both understand the references made in advertising campaigns as well as be attracted to the church because of them. To the pastor and his creative team, city residents are thought to be well acquainted with pop culture, to engage in and enjoy high-tech media, and to be creative, artistic, educated, fast-paced, and cool (Lloyd 2006). This imagery, needless to say, is often quite removed from the socially conservative religious and cultural traditions that many associate with white Evangelicalism. Nonetheless, it is deeply enmeshed in the urban imaginary that animates DC's leadership, as the following anecdote from Barron's field notes makes clear:

After the Sunday evening service let out, I was standing out in the lobby area off to the side, away from the heavy [foot] traffic. Pastor Phil came up to me and asked me how I liked the service. After some small talk, Pastor Phil begins to point out various people around the lobby. He points out a fair-skinned black woman with a large red afro and says, "I just love her look, she is so artistic and that's what we like here." He then turns his attention to two other women who appeared to be Latina and claims they are in school and young professionals. He described them as "real go-getters." He makes the point to tell me that they had a lot of people who were in college or up-and-coming professionals, "You know, 'cause that is what Chicago is, on-the-go young people." He then points out a couple more men and women and gives me a blurb about their appearance, style, where they went to school in the city, their credentials, and professional life. He smiles as his chest swells a bit, almost with a sense of pride as he

ran down the line of credentials among his congregants. He ended by saying, "And you, I love the fact that you have a nose ring and you are going to be a doctor. You have a very unique look and that is something we embrace here. I mean that's what the city of Chicago is all about."
—Field note

Pastor Phil seemed clearly happy with what he perceived as DC's success in drawing the right type of people. They are educated and creative, launching into or becoming successful in career or school, and in his view quite fashion forward. He is also quite clearly aligning individuals' personal qualities with their dress and appearance—their public display of themselves is taken as indicative of their personhood. This isn't a congregation for "losers," Pastor Phil seems to be implying, it is where the "cool kids" are coming to church.

Saving Chicago, Becoming Chicago

Several times we heard Downtown Church leaders claim that they intentionally chose one of the youngest cities in the country with regard to demographics in which to plant the new congregation, and they also claimed that it was one of the most unchurched.

> You know, Chicago is one of the top three youngest cities in the country, it's also the most unchurched city in the country. There are more liquor stores in this city than there are churches. Our goal here at Downtown Church is to provide those people with a place to go and feel comfortable, a place unlike any other church in the city.
> —Pastor Phil, Sunday evening service

This statement, although not fully accurate statistically,[1] not only reflects an image of Chicago but also reflects a common understanding of urban centers held by religious organizations that originate outside the city, particularly among American Protestants. These images have been common since the early twentieth century (Orsi 1999; Ammerman 1997). The interpretations of the urban world by those who come from outside it understand population density and heterogeneity to encourage a freedom from social and spiritual restraint (Orsi 1999). Moral sensationalism about sinful cities has a long tradition in American culture (Williams 2002) and especially in the Midwest (Williams 2004). Chicago, in fact, has a popular culture mythology of being "trouble" (Boehm 2004)—whether its nineteenth-century ethnic and political tensions (such as the Haymarket "riot"), or the Prohibition-era violence connected to bootlegging and Al Capone. This history and mythology have provoked outsiders to enter urban landscapes to reform and spiritually revive their inhabitants. Downtown Church partially deviates from this agenda in its approach to the city in that its charge is not solely reformative but also a bit celebratory. This reflects, above all, its desires to be seen as authentic—"the *real* church for the city, unlike any other church here."

This rationale for founding DC in an "unchurched" city conveniently ignores that the Chicago location is not far from the Indiana home of the Big Church, the foundational resource base for the new church. In that way, Pastor Phil and his team are claiming a motivational narrative independent of Phil's father and the home church. But also, claiming that Chicago "needs" this type of ministry fails to acknowledge the extent to which Pastor Phil and his leadership team were working with a glamorized idea of what constitutes the "big city" and a diverse, metropolitan constituency. Moreover, even if not a stated goal, starting a campus of the Big Church in a large city could work to extend its brand. And Chicago is close enough to "home" so that resources can be shared and the Big Church can still maintain an influential role in the development of its franchise. But these factors are underplayed in the DC narrative. One can imagine that Pastor Phil must manage a balancing act between his desire to build a particular type of congregation and his father's expectations related to the expansion of the Big Church.

In its marketing schemes, in claims made in sermons, and in creative team meetings, Downtown Church asserts that it is the true church for the city of Chicago; it is the "authentic" urban-based church *in* the city of Chicago and *for* the city of Chicago. The claim to be an authentically urban church is essential for Downtown Church in its effort to associate itself with those it regards as authentic members of Chicago's urban community. These authentic members are imagined to be young professionals, well-educated, and worldly. The pursuit of this version of authenticity also sets the congregation apart from neighboring competitor churches who might be vying for the same demographic and target location in downtown Chicago. Affirmations of authenticity come through the use of a central urban location (Marti 2005, 2008), incorporation of a middle-class consumer lifestyle centered on the city (Zukin 1993, 1995; Greenberg 2008), and the visible presence of what various urban-based churches consider the urban essence—racial and ethnic diversity (Wilson 1996; Wacquant and Wilson 1999; Marti 2005; Edwards 2008).

Downtown Church meets for worship only on Sunday evenings in a rented performing arts theater in the greater downtown area of Chicago. The theater is mere blocks away from the city's upscale restaurants, lounges, and bars, and only a mile or so from the city's downtown core, the Loop. Between areas known as the West Loop and the South Loop, the church is surrounded by racially diverse neighborhoods, several of which are gentrifying. New city residents and middle-class consumers can enjoy amenities such as factories converted into condos and innovative ethnic fusion restaurants. The destruction of nearby low-income housing also put gentrified black neighborhoods in close proximity to the congregation (Pattillo-McCoy 1999, 2007).

Downtown Church is thus intended to emulate a "non-church" atmosphere and to create an alternative space to appeal to upwardly mobile, college-educated young adults, a group currently less represented within white evangelical Protestantism (Flory and Miller 2008). Its endeavor is consistent with an effort that came out of evangelical efforts in the mid-1990s that was dubbed the Emergent Church Movement (ECM). Evangelical Protestantism has placed less emphasis on ritual and liturgical tradition and more on experiential and emotional participation. The ECM continued that move (Flory and Miller 2008; Marti and Ganiel 2014). In spite of this structural distancing, the vast majority of these emergent churches have remained steadfast in their conservative values, framed within a white middle-class sensibility. Youth who grew up amid the ECM may now see that approach as "traditional," and are looking for even more alternative "non-church" options. Like many Americans exposed to features of highly globalized, pluralistic, postmodern society, spiritual individualism puts tradition on shaky ground for college-educated evangelicals; many young evangelicals find themselves stuck between tradition and innovation.

One can see these tensions in Downtown Church, where congregants enjoy concert-like worship services, as well as unorthodox sermons related to the latest trends in social media and pop culture. However, the order of service, music style, and music selections are generally in keeping with traditionally white evangelical congregations, and not very different from the Big Church's practices. Downtown Church is considered nondenominational evangelical Protestant, and echoes the deep history of innovative evangelical efforts to confront and convert worldly society, even as it often cherishes its own traditions.

It is also important to recognize that city residents are not understood to be highly religious by the DC leadership teams. The descriptions of those who are "unchurched" used by the pastor and his creative team incorporate those who have stepped away from church but are on their way back, those who don't have time for church, and those who don't have a place to attend that meets the needs of their "city life." Many unchurched Americans have become disillusioned by organized religion, and their disaffection is fueled by the perception that religion has been hypocritical, corrupt, and an ethical failure (Flory and Miller 2008). However, unchurched people represent a vital resource needed for religious institutions to remain viable, steady, and influential, as many American congregations are aging (Chaves 2004; Flory and Miller 2008). Further, converting those not already in the faith is one of the definitional aspects of evangelical religion. Thus, the unchurched are often seen as a "mission field."

However, while Downtown Church is geared toward the young urbanite living in a racially diverse, metropolitan city, the distance of the majority of the pastoral leadership and the creative team living in homogeneous neighborhoods in nearby Indiana creates a regional and racial disconnect between the leadership staff and many of those among its racially diverse membership. This disconnect leads the leadership staff to rely on stereotypical tropes of authenticity found in the racialization of urban space (Johnson 2003; Grazian 2004). Church leaders began to develop their racialized urban imaginary—a conceptual framework used to navigate this unfamiliar territory—as they began to engage their perceptions of and expectations for residents of Chicago. Class and racial homogeneity among creative team leaders is perhaps the basis for a shared imaginary that shapes their goals and informs their organizational processes.

Borders, Boundaries, and the Leadership Team

Below the creative team on Downtown Church's organizational chart are other members drawn from the Big Church who came to join the church planting efforts. They are women and men who were involved in second-tier positions at the Big Church, such as greet staff and vocalists on the worship team, but they were all involved with and understand the elaborate worship productions put on by the Big Church. They hope to bring some of that dramatic flair to the big city of Chicago. These men and women are called the *leadership team*, which began as subordinate to the creative team. However, as the church has grown, these two teams have begun to overlap with each other in both personnel and in responsibilities. As new members from Chicago began to join Downtown Church, Phil hand-picked a few members to join the leadership team and the creative team, and also invited one "city couple" to join the ruling Elder Board. Those on the leadership team at times can offer suggestions and input into the development of the congregation, but they essentially function as managers of departments (or teams) within the organization. However, given that many of the members of the creative and leadership teams continue to work at, and live near, the Big Church in Indiana, tensions often arise between "city" and "suburb" ways of doing ministry. Both leaders and congregants of Downtown Church envision their congregation as a space for the entire city of Chicago, not simply part of it. On one hand, this opens the church to a wide variety of people; but on the other hand, when the boundaries become fluid it creates contested expectations of belonging and church direction.

For example, the creative team and leadership staff do not consider themselves to be outsiders to the city of Chicago, at least not completely. Pastor Phil moved to Royal Oaks, an affluent Chicago neighborhood, about a year-and-a-half after he started Downtown Church. However, he is still a full-time pastor at his father's church, and he still owns a home in Indiana. He and his family stay multiple days out of the week in Indiana while he and Emily work at the Big Church. Further, the overwhelming majority of the creative team personnel who first began with the church still lives in Indiana and is still employed by the Big Church. Nonetheless, they wholeheartedly consider their community in Indiana a "suburb of Chicago." In a dozen sermons that referenced the Big

Church, Pastor Phil has even referred to the suburb of Indiana where his father's church is located as the "greater Chicagoland area."

The town in which the Big Church is located is pretty well outside of the nearest south suburb of Chicago, making its self-designation as a suburb highly contested among congregants. While Chicago is certainly the major orienting metropolitan city and media market for this part of Indiana, most would probably consider the town as falling outside of the greater Chicagoland area. Calling it Chicagoland actually annoys some DC members who are Chicago city residents. I sat down in the church lobby with Lauren, one of the newly appointed leaders at Downtown Church. She is not from the Big Church and resides in a Chicago neighborhood not far from DC. She is one of five other new Chicago-based leaders who have been recently appointed. Their positions are all voluntary.

> We sat down at one of the high two-seater tables placed all throughout the lobby [of the theater the church uses for its services]. It was a weekday and so no one from the church was around. She requested we meet at the church since it was close to her gym and she had a workout planned shortly after. She is in her late twenties, has her M.A. and describes herself as a successful businesswoman. There were security guards and staff from the theater getting the lobby ready for one of the weekly productions going on later that night. I asked her about the relationship between Downtown Church and the Big Church and she began to discuss the "suburb of Chicago comment" right away. "No are you kidding, I would never consider them [the Big Church] in the greater Chicagoland area or a suburb of Chicago. Anything that is 45 miles away is far away, that just doesn't make sense. I am from Chicago, not the suburbs, and I don't consider anyone that lives where they are from to live in Chicago, and see that's the problem, they think they [leadership staff] are from here and they aren't."
> —Field note

Lauren made a clear distinction regarding who has the right to claim a local identity. She is a Chicago resident and for her, the boundaries of identity are geographically tied to the city limits. Her statement revealed a conflict in identity politics based on a conception of geographic boundaries. Valerie, the only non–Indiana based elder on the board at Downtown Church, shared similar sentiments. I met Valerie in the church offices for an interview. It was early on a Saturday morning. Valerie is a 42-year-old black woman who grew up in Chicago and is now a lawyer involved in the political scene in the city. The statements about the geographic relationship between Chicago and the Big Church came up, to which she responded, "people from Chicago are kind of like, Indiana is, uh [laughter] let's just say by no means have we ever considered any part of Indiana to be a part of us."

These differing views of who belongs to the city call into question the power to name and identify. How do these distinctions affect the church's identity? Even though the pastor recently moved to Royal Oaks, for many congregants that did not buy him a pass into authentic residency. Many members still view him as a suburban resident due to his continuing involvement with the Big Church. These symbolic boundaries hold identity value for the Chicago residents. Members such as Lauren think of themselves as city dwellers and do not want to be associated with a suburban identity. The distinction also implies a value hierarchy. Each group asserts its own capacity to define boundaries based on its residential status. The city dwellers claim that they know what is suburban and what is urban. And the suburban leadership and now locally based Pastor Phil claim that they have a handle on the city because they imagine its boundaries to incorporate their town. Conversely, those who live in the city of Chicago view themselves as holding the authority to define what an authentic church in and for the city of Chicago should look like.

Residential status isn't the only thing that separates the leadership from many members. It is clear on Sundays which group is which by the way they arrive at the church for worship services. Those who live in the city are dropped off by the city bus a block away, or walk from the nearest train stop. Others drive and search for parking in the lot across the street—not always easy even on a Sunday. By contrast, the leaders from the Big Church arrive together in a group. Every Sunday, like clockwork, a caravan of cars, complete with drivers, pulls up to the front of the theater to drop off the pastor and his leadership team from the Big Church.

It's 4:45 p.m. and there is a row of five cars lined up in front of the theater. There are two BMW sports cars, two Mercedes Benz luxury sedans, and a large SUV. Each car has a driver. These drivers are interns from the Big Church. The pastor and his family have their own car. The rest of the cars have a mixture of different people on the leadership team. There are 12 people that arrive, five women and seven men. The men wear designer jeans and shirts, with the logos and brand names on visible display. All of the women wear high heels and hold designer purses. Each of the women has a combination of heavy makeup and large jewelry that sparkles in the sunlight. The group of 12 comes through the double doors in a rush. Some are on their phones; others are spouting off orders to the volunteers who are waiting for them at the door. The women are loud, laughing and talking. Three of the men greeted some of the volunteers with a handshake, asking them about their week while quickly moving on to the next person. Three of the women rush to the back of the theater, telling the other women that they must go to the bathroom to fix their hair and makeup, from their long drive.

—Field note

The volunteers and congregants already at the church were not dressed the same way as those in the caravan. The volunteers are fashionably dressed but more subtle in their attire. The women did not have heavy makeup or large designer bags, and only one of the volunteers was wearing heels. A woman commented, "Whenever they [pastoral staff] come, I feel like it's European fashion week up in here." The other volunteers laugh, continuing to talk about how different their dress was from the leaders. They commented on all of the designer labels, heels, and makeup: "I can't wear all that and then try to catch the train. I'd bust my face trying to get on in those heels and then get jacked (laughter)."

The distinctions in arrival and dress display different orientations to the city. The city-based volunteers saw the suburban leaders as separated by clothing and self-presentation, partly the result of not having to ride public transportation, as many do in the city. The boundaries seem set upon arrival at church. The caravan offers a clear distinction of group and locational standpoint that each group brings to the church. Furthermore, members of the caravan even indicate that their ride is long, inadvertently alluding to the possibility that the Big Church falls outside of the bounds of the city.

Consequently, various members assert that the pastor and his creative team do not have the ability to create the type of church they desire, due to their outsider perspective:

> Honestly I don't think people from Indiana understand Chicago. I think people have a stereotype of what Chicago is. It's hip, fast, and it's some of that, but Chicago is a grounded city, we are still in the Midwest. They think it is the media and the lights and the way people dress and it's some of that, but I always laugh when they walk in because we don't wear that here in the city. I just don't think he [Pastor Phil] knows what it means to be a church in the city.
> —Valerie, black congregant

However, conversations with members and congregational leaders reveal that more than one-third of the congregation consists of transplants to Chicago, with a large majority of those relocating within the last five years. Sixty percent of the people interviewed had moved to Chicago from cities and suburbs across the Midwest, and very few had lived previously in a metropolitan city like Chicago. Interestingly, they also indicated often that their ties to their previous homes in suburbs and other cities were not particularly strong (or work and school make their schedules too tight), and they only visit there a couple times a year. One result is that these transplants have shifted their allegiances and identities and view themselves as official urban dwellers. Many of them imagined, just as the congregational leadership team did, that Chicago had a fast pace, economic and social opportunity, and a cosmopolitan lifestyle that was not available in their home cities such as Lincoln, Nebraska, Des Moines, Iowa, or even Detroit, Michigan. Thus, the leaders and many members share similar imaginations of Chicago as a city. Additionally, the presence of these transplanted members in the church reinforces the pastor's notion of Chicago being a place of young, single, go-getters. The assessments by both the leadership and new transplanted members support each other, even as they clash with the views of many of the long-time Chicago residents.

Valerie also went on to say that she did not believe the pastor knew his place in the city and because of that she did not know the church's place in the city. She didn't view Pastor Phil as someone who really understood the city of Chicago, even though he had recently moved there. For her, Royal Oaks isn't a fair representation of the diversity of the city, and she lamented that it limited his scope. For Valerie, the constant back-and-forth between the Big Church and Downtown Church does not offer the pastor the ability to understand what life in the city really is and, as a result, where and how Downtown Church should orient itself.

Nonetheless, the pastoral leadership has a quite definitive and clear vision of the city, as a wide-ranging, if somewhat disjointed, interview with one of the members of the creative team, Assistant Pastor Paul, clearly revealed. Pastor Paul is also one of Pastor Phil's closest friends. One afternoon, I met him in the church office adjacent to the theater. As I entered, Paul was walking rapidly throughout the office, shouting out greetings to volunteers, talking on the phone, and engaging in sidebar conversations with others in the office. Repeatedly throughout the interview, Paul answered his phone, responded to incoming texts, and left the room to give more instructions to the volunteers. The impression was certainly one of energy, pace, drive, and authority.

During the course of the interview, Paul repeatedly referenced being a church in the city, and when asked to elaborate on what that meant, responded:

> Well, I can't really tell you what "urban" is just yet but I can tell you what it's not, it's not the suburbs. People have other things going on than just the church. They don't have Little League and Bible study. They have other things going on so they can't be at church every night. We want our church to represent the city of Chicago. So what is the city of Chicago? On one block you got projects, on the next block you have million-dollar high rises. In the city of Chicago you have low-income housing living next to rulers of the world. So we want that scope, those that have an urban mind-set, that are in the urban flow, that are cultured and connected. We want to create that community.

This is an interesting description of the city, both explicitly and implicitly contrasting it to the suburbs. In Pastor Paul's mind, these are two different places where residents' lifestyles will not fit together and where the residents have different needs. Pastor Paul notes the ways in which the suburban church can be the center of social and family life, opportunities which he believes are not available in the city. Pastor Paul notes the diversity—social and economic—of the city, clearly implying a homogeneity of the suburbs. He indicates that Downtown Church wants members who are in the "urban flow" and are "cultured and connected," again a seeming contrast to the staid conformity of suburban life. The place, whether urban or suburban, seems itself to generate different needs, people, and churches. Suburbs assume children and traditional family life. Urban assumes culture, distractions, and "flow." Further, Paul's sweeping economic distinctions described the city as a place of close proximity of difference and diversity, which in turn produces energy and excitement for the church and its developers. Paul's statement juxtaposing housing projects with millionaire mansions generally ignores the city's residential segregation, though it does call to mind one notable example—the fact that the economically upper-crust "Gold Coast" along Lake Michigan is only a mile from where the Cabrini-Green housing projects once stood. This contrast has engaged the imagination of other social scientists (Wellman 1999; Price 2000) and is an effective symbol of contrasting socioeconomic fortunes. It is, however, the exception in the city, not the norm.

Marti (2005:58) states, "a person initially becomes a part of a congregation because he or she sees it as something that fits with some element of himself or herself." The corporate identity Downtown Church wants to foster is that of a young urban dweller, who is educated, professional, and either completely new to the faith, or has stepped away from traditional Christian churches and is on the way back, looking for something different. For many members, Downtown Church is a church that can help them to understand their place in this world as an urbanite and as a Christian—a set of contradictory identities in the minds of many evangelical Protestants and many secular urbanites. Many members sought out Downtown Church as something new and different that they hoped could address the reality of their lives, especially those not following more conventional paths found in middle-class suburban Christianity—getting married (often somewhat young), having children early, and settling down (Flory and Miller 2008). Yet some members have come to realize that Downtown Church may be ill-equipped to follow through on this promise, as the congregation remains heavily resourced by the Big Church. One result is that many aspects of the suburban mega-church model, and its assumptions about programming, spill over into the development of Downtown Church.

> It was brought to my attention that Pastor Phil and Kyle [another leader] are from an "event driven" church, you know, 'cause of his dad's church. They come from that suburban mega-church model of big productions. But, we have all of these things here in the city, so we don't need to get it from the church. We don't need productions; we have the city. We need the basics. Not a big program, 'cause I don't have time for that, just tell me how to live my life day to day. I don't need a production.
> —Linda, white congregant

Although Linda and other members express dissatisfaction with some of the programming efforts, they still attend Downtown Church, and in Linda's case, get involved in leadership. Members may not agree with the conceptualization of what is appropriate for a church in a city, but they appreciate the efforts of a church attempting to meet their needs.

Volunteer Team: Not Too Black, Not Too White

Operating under the creative team and the leadership team on the organizational flowchart are the *volunteer teams*. These are comprised of unpaid positions, and are occupied by new members of the Downtown Church congregation, that is, those who reside within the city of Chicago and hence are not transfers from the Big Church. Mostly new to ministry in any capacity, volunteer leaders are nonetheless responsible for much of the daily operations of the congregation, in addition to running the weekly service. Given that the majority of the leadership and creative teams are still full-time staff in the Big Church, and most still live in Indiana, the volunteer teams do DC's on-the-ground work. Unlike the creative and leadership teams, the volunteer staff is racially diverse, but with minimal class diversity. There are also more women on the volunteer teams than the other teams.

While members of the volunteer teams do not get paid, and are usually not in any fundamental decision-making capacity, they are integral to Downtown Church's public identity. The ethno-racial diversity among the volunteer teams is crucial for sustaining the claim that the church is "of" the city and that it represents all of the various people who make up the city of Chicago. In a sense, the volunteer team members constitute the church's self-proclaimed identity as diverse. The pastoral leadership recognizes this, although often only implicitly. For example, one Assistant Pastor responded in part to a question about Downtown Church's competition among congregations in the city:

> No, those other churches out there aren't like us. We are really a church for the city. Other churches can be real vanilla, but that's not us. I mean, look around. We have people from everywhere, all over Europe, Latin America, black guys, white guys. Other places are just white, just plain ol' white.
> —Assistant Pastor Craig

Being "really a church for the city" and being ethno-racially diverse are almost synonymous here, with Pastor Craig using one concept following the other in adjacent sentences. Interestingly, however, Pastor Phil rarely ever explicitly mentions race or racial diversity as a component of the congregation or as a goal for Downtown Church to achieve. Note the conversation reported earlier in which he discussed the "look" displayed by various members, or their professions or vocations. Conversations with both pastors and congregants had respondents describing their church as "diverse," although without necessarily articulating what type of diversity that might be. Assistant Pastor Craig contrasts the DC congregation with "vanilla" or "plain ol' white" but lists origins in Europe and Latin America as signs of diversity, before getting to "black guys" and "white guys."

According to responses from interviews with the pastoral staff, Downtown Church is approximately 75% white.[2] Asian (8%) and Latino/a members (7%) are the largest minority groups in these estimates, while African American (6%) and multiracial (4%) members are represented in smaller numbers. As we have seen, sociological research on multiracial and multi-ethnic congregations generally use 80% as the definitional cut-off number—if 80% of church members are from the same ethno-racial group, the congregation cannot be considered "multiracial" (see Emerson, Edwards, Marti, Garcas-Foley 2008). By that measure, Downtown Church would qualify as multiracial, although just barely, and at some points has undoubtedly been 80% white. Yet while Downtown Church is proud of its diversity, it does not present itself as "multiracial," nor does it articulate that status or a process of "racial reconciliation" as self-conscious congregational goals.

One identity goal that Downtown Church is more explicit about, however, works in the other direction. DC leaders are quite clear that they do not want to be recognized or identified as a "black church." Assistant Pastor Craig explained:

> We don't want to be a "black church." There are already churches like that so we have to be careful about how we set up our church so it doesn't go that way. We want to keep the "downtown" vibe.

The pastoral staff at other points expressed some concern that they not be misrepresented as an "inner-city" church rather than a "downtown" one. This distinction seems to draw on the common American use of "inner-city" as a substitute for "poverty" or "ghetto" and an implicit synonym for African American. Certainly for Downtown Church the concern seems a bit overstated. The percentage of African American members is small, the church community is most attractive and accessible to middle-class groups, and physically it is at some distance from Chicago's poorest and most dangerous neighborhoods. Conceptual categories such as "downtown," or "inner-city"—even a "black church"—are ambiguous, but they have clear folk meanings that draw from the larger conception of the city—cities in general and Chicago in particular—as tightly connected to its black population.

In some ways, it is not surprising that Chicago in particular has this deep cultural connection to African American life. Chicago was a major destination of the "Great Migration" of African Americans from the American South to the industrializing cities of the north from 1920 to 1970. Several of Jacob Lawrence's paintings in his magisterial "Migration" series focus on Chicago. The development of blues music, particularly its electrified form, happened in clubs in Chicago, by many of those who came north during the Great Migration. A major work of early American sociology was specifically about Chicago's black community, St. Clair Drake and Horace Cayton's *Black Metropolis*, first published in 1945. And of course, the nation's first black president called Chicago home. Thus, while urban scholars such as Larry Bennett (2010) see Chicago as being three distinct cities in three different political and economic eras, each of these has been deeply etched by African American culture and politics. At the same time, as many scholars and journalists have noted (e.g., Boehm 2004; Sampson 2013), the city has a long history of segregation and racial tension, often marked by violence.

Assistant Pastor Craig followed up his comment above by expanding on his distinction between "downtown" and "inner-city":

> You know, we are more like a "city" church, you know, located in the downtown area where everything is going on. We are not an "inner-city" church, no way. Those churches serve people with different needs than our congregation. We are more of a "downtown" church, you know, right in the center of downtown life.

As he scrambles to define what it means to be a city church, "downtown" comes up almost like a mantra. In his enthusiasm for the idea of "downtown," one can almost hear the words from Petula Clark's 1964 pop hit, "Downtown": "The lights are much brighter there, You can forget all your troubles, forget all your cares, And go downtown, things will be great when you're downtown." It sounds cheery and excited, with a naïve enthusiasm about where the action is. And it is determined not to associate the church with inequality, social problems, or other urban ills. Yet the racial and non-racialized conceptions of "downtown" and "inner-city" again collided when Craig was then asked to elaborate on the differences between inner-city and downtown churches in Chicago. His response provided the names of predominantly black congregations in distressed neighborhoods on the city's South Side. Thus, his distinctions played with ambiguity, but combined both racialized and classed meanings and were clearly influenced by the historic economic disadvantage of black Americans in urban centers generally and Chicago in particular (Massey and Denton 1993).

Leaders of Downtown Church believe their success in the urban religious market depends heavily on their ability to attract the consumer class of young professionals, without acquiring the stigma that is often associated with the poor racial minorities who live in parts of the city. In a sense, they want to take advantage of the commodification of urban blackness (Grazian 2004; hooks 1993; Johnson 2003) that has made it culturally popular and often cutting-edge. But to do this they must control the extent to which black members, or black religious culture, actually define the church. In the same way, many of the racial politics within Downtown Church are influenced by the negotiation and appropriation of blackness on the part of church leaders, often with the complicity of congregants. Like many nightclubs, restaurants, and other urban establishments, Downtown Church engages in a form of racially charged cultural production and cultural consumption. This cultural production and consumption relies on the racialization of the urban landscape (Grazian 2004, 2007) and images and history that connect with a consumerist approach to the city. Downtown Church is set within a broader context and religious tradition that is marked by organizational competition and what would now be called "branding." But there is also a long narrative of ideological inclusion ("all are welcome"), often combined with social exclusion, which challenges evangelical Protestant church organizations as they try to acquire membership in an unfamiliar urban environment.

A Church in the City: The Power of Place

Downtown Church targets young adults, often as they experience a transitional period in their lives establishing adult and career identities, and often in a new place. It does so by trying to offer something that can be seen as new and exciting, and that can be enjoyed in the same way that other aspects of urban culture can be consumed. All of this "culture work," however, is on the margins—on the edge of evangelical Protestantism's approach to the city (as opposed to small-town or suburban life), on the edge of conservative religious approaches to sex and marriage, on the edge of racial homogeneity and diversity. These boundaries used by the leaders, the volunteers, and the members bring to the forefront various ways of imagining the city.

Border Wars

"A community exists only insofar as it exists in peoples' minds . . . there must be some shared conception, however rough, of a demarcated place providing common identification and shared interests" (Molotch 1972:4). Though prior research has shown that racial identity and religious leaders are key in shaping congregational identity, we know considerably less about the ways in which racialized contexts, particularly about place, may influence religious leaders' views of congregant desirability, or how this influence may shape dynamics within a congregation. Differences in conceptions of the ideal church, along with the larger ideological positions within which such conceptions are held, can produce conflict, revealing the politics of the congregation's authority.

Part of the contention within Downtown Church comes from a great divergence in the degree to which DC leaders are accepted by new and potential members as an integral part of the Chicago landscape. As we have seen, much of the pastoral staff, and members who are long-time Chicago residents, do not share the same conceptual map of Chicago and how DC should be positioned on it. This conceptual landscape is ambiguous for many, and all versions rest on the ability of DC to claim membership in this "club" of Chicago urbanites. As these imaginaries shape the goals that church leaders are attempting to accomplish, they also affect how the plans to achieve the goals are executed. Throughout our exploration of Downtown Church, we find that the process by which people determine the boundaries that differentiate their geographical and social worlds has consequences for inclusion and exclusion of groups of people, and the organizational practices that in fact are the church itself.

Borders and Bloodlines

The distinction made about origins is important to consider when understanding Downtown Church. Congregations, like other groups of humans, operate with a set of cultural and social conventions (Becker 1982). Some of these must appease their governing bodies (such as a denomination, or the founding church), and some of these must appease their target consumers. The freedom or restriction within these conventions will affect the type of cultural objects—whether worship services or social identities—that are produced for distribution. Congregations are a product of a larger system of religious institutions. These institutions possess a body of conventional understandings about common practices, rituals, materials, and beliefs. While in many ways Pastor Phil is attempting to create his own congregation, set apart from the goals of his father's church, the effort is accompanied by people and conventions that share direct ties to the Big Church. Their allegiance to the Big Church shapes their conceptualizations of ministry, Chicago's borders, and their place in the city. The Big Church assumes that Downtown Church will be an extension of its ministry, but Downtown Church doesn't necessarily see it that way. It may be a church "plant," but the metaphorical soil is different.

At the same time, congregational identity is also shaped "from below" by the social characteristics of participants, even as it responds to pressures "from above" emanating from the denominations and religious traditions in which the congregations are embedded (Chaves 2004). Thus, understanding how a congregation is conceptualized is vital to understanding congregational life. Downtown Church is not only a cultural object produced by the Big Church but is also composed of people who are themselves cultural producers and who are imagining a particular product for the consumption of—and consumption by—the city. Cities are potential sites for spiritual revival and are also centers for cultural reproduction, in which cultural industries and the urban market negotiate and reproduce cultural identities (Zukin 1995). Downtown Church leaders are navigating through these cultural cues in order to understand how to consume the city and in turn how to produce a cultural object to be consumed in Chicago. Church leaders move away from the goals of the Big Church while shedding, embracing, and transforming their suburban, Indiana identity.

Race, Place, and Identity

While congregational research has shown that racial identity and religious leaders' intentional efforts are central to shaping race relations within a congregation (e.g., Edwards 2008), we know considerably less about the ways in which racialized contexts influence religious leaders' views of race relations, or how this influence may shape race relations within a congregation. Church leaders engage their racialized urban imaginary as they construct narratives about suburban and urban places across racial lines. Downtown Church leaders have responded to the cultural connections between black Americans and Chicago by advancing an urban, but non-black, religious identity.

Through the racialization of public place, the built environment becomes a landscape riddled with racially coded symbolic meanings. Racially coded themes become translated into universal truths, naturalized over time, and reflect the power of the racial structures that organize American society. In the same breath, church leaders recognize the distinctive diversity in the city that makes Chicago so appealing to them and articulate the desire to resist a black identity. This particular form of embracing the city's diversity has a paradoxical effect on congregational goals. Church leaders have not only selected "one of the youngest cities" in which to work, but also a city that is notorious for its marked racial and class segregation. As church leaders attempt to attract congregants who themselves have more exposure to racial and class diversity than do many in the leadership, they will continue to traverse borders in complex and contradictory ways.

In the politics of the imaginary, the intersection of race and place is where Downtown Church legitimates its presence in the city. The next chapter illustrates how the pastoral staff, as cultural producers, manufactures and promotes authenticity through gendered, raced, and class-based assumptions of the city. This is evident in their advertising campaigns, web content, worship space, and sermons. In an effort to attract congregants, they first imagine them as middle-class consumers. Church leaders then simultaneously offer a space that reaffirms a city lifestyle (enticing to young attendees who are disconnected from traditional church settings) and engages in actions that constitute and reproduce social inequality within their congregation.

2

Urban Outfitters

I went inside and there's a bar. I was like, wow, can I order a drink and sit down, you know? It seemed like a club
atmosphere.
—Crystal, black congregant

Downtown church is dedicated to attracting young, single, and "on-
the-go" urban dwellers looking to blend their city lives and religious
faith. In an effort to do so, Downtown Church engages in unconventional marketing schemes and uses non-traditional spaces of
worship. At the core of Downtown Church is a "matrix of authenticity" triangulated by middle-class consumption of city spaces, urban
nightlife and entertainment, and the visible presence of racial and
ethnic minorities thought to characterize the "diversity" that marks
a city. Becoming an authentic Chicago church—at least in the view
of Downtown Church—is a matter of enticing the senses. It aims
to accomplish this goal by fostering an entertainment-oriented
aura for the worship services while filling the church with people
who embody the type of trendy, affluent, and multiracial identities
thought typical of a hip urban center. To investigate how this matrix
operates, we illustrate how the pastoral staff, acting as the producers
of their congregational culture, manufacture and enact this version
of authenticity through gendered, raced, and class-based assumptions
of city life. These expectations become manifest in their congregational advertising campaigns, worship space, church policies, and
sermonizing. Downtown Church leaders engage in practices typically associated with seducing the urban consumer, simultaneously
offering a space that reaffirms a city lifestyle while engaging in organizational practices that ultimately constitute and reproduce social
inequality.

Branding the Matrix

Our post-industrial urban economy is heavily dependent upon retail sales and consumer spending. Engaging the consumer with the "experience" of the city is crucial to marketing and thus sales. Downtown retail and entertainment areas in particular are concerned with experiential marketing through trendsetting individuality, exciting architectural designs, and enticing imagery. Culture consumers, particularly from educated middle and professional classes, are drawn to this production of symbols and space, consuming and ultimately reproducing this version of the city as a public culture. When retail and experience are the economic engines in the contemporary urban economy, cultural producers create marketing schemes that seek to encourage consumption practices modeled on the imagined lifestyle of a particular demographic—in this case, the highly prized young professionals with disposable income and discerning cultural tastes that crave distinction (Grazian 2007; Lloyd 2006; Mele 2000; Zukin 1993). The marketplace thus produces a racialized urban imagination that explicitly incorporates a diverse consumer body but implicitly reproduces structures of inequality on the axes of class, gender, and race.

Designer Church

Today I am running late. Luckily the bus is running late as well. I hop on the bus and head downtown. I'm able to locate a vacant seat, a rarity for a weekend bus at this time. In an effort to not break rule number one of public transit and make eye contact with a fellow passenger, I begin to scan all of the advertisements running along the perimeter of the bus walls. Then I spot it, an advertisement for Downtown Church. The ad has a red backdrop with a large handbag in the middle. The slogan reads, *DESIGNER CHURCH* in gold. The handbag is nearly identical to a handbag featured in a new international ad campaign released by a well-known designer label. The church's address reads across one line at the bottom of the sign in gold print. In the upper right-hand corner is a small Scripture reference, however due to the

border frame of the advertising space, the verse cannot be
completely made out.
—Field note

In an effort to attract their ideal member, Downtown Church sets up
various marketing campaigns throughout the city of Chicago, treating
potential members as retail consumers. Their advertisements are found
on buses, trains, mailers, and flyers all over the downtown area. The
Designer Church theme highlights a type of glamorous, leisure-driven
lifestyle in place of significantly referencing traditional religious markers or denominational associations. By associating the church with a
high-end brand, the ads assert that Downtown Church is distinctive
and exclusive. Calling itself a designer church communicates the congregation's departure from many popular conventions and images
of American Christianity, particularly those that would distance the
church from "the world" dominated by secular understandings and
concern with material life. The message couldn't be farther from the
somber asceticism often associated with Protestantism. Rather, Downtown Church embraces the intertwining of the church with a particular
slice of the world—the successful, young, rising in affluence, urban
dweller.

For example, another manifestation of the Downtown Church
marketing campaign targets those familiar with urban nightlife and
entertainment:

> Standing at one of the "L" stops, I see a large advertisement for Down-
> town Church. Featured in the center of the ad is a tilted martini glass.
> Underneath the glass it reads ABSOLUTE CHURCH—a play on the
> vodka company Absolut, and its recent ad campaign. There is a Scripture
> reference in the top left-hand corner that refers to Jesus quenching your
> thirst. At the bottom of the advertisement are the name of the church, the
> meeting place, and the time of the Sunday service.
> —Field note

Absolute Church is a provocative attempt to capitalize on an audience
of consumers seeking a certain kind of experience—a night out full of
cocktails and fun. It is a direct rejection of the teetotaling past associated

with evangelical Protestantism. One could potentially read the ad as suggesting that the church could fill the needs and quench the thirsts that people currently seek when they turn to alcohol. But the picture and the tone of the ad encourage a different interpretation—one in which the church wants to *associate* itself with the glamour of the brand and the lifestyle that would lead people to be familiar with the vodka and the ad campaign. In *On the Make*, David Grazian (2007) argued that downtown areas in cities foster a space for a particular stage in the life cycle—prolonged adolescence. Given the consumer economy and the rise in educational attainment, cultural producers capitalize on the marketing schemes and consumption practices associated with a prolonged adolescence to develop the urban nightlife scene. Grazian (2007) claims that, with the help of cultural entrepreneurs such as creative marketers and cultural laborers, urban nightlife settings create a place that offers what he calls the "nocturnal experience." A lucrative and now staple feature of downtown areas of a city, the nocturnal experience is an essential component to the culture of a thriving city. Downtown Church capitalizes on this move by extending the experience to church. Downtown Church sends this message in ways beyond its advertising images; for example, its services are in a rented performing arts theater in the downtown area of Chicago. It is not unusual at all, of course, for start-up early churches to use rented storefronts, but not surprisingly they are usually small stores in retail areas a bit more "down in the heels." Downtown Church is in a performing arts building just blocks away from bars, clubs, and restaurants. Further, the church holds its weekly service every Sunday evening at 5:30 p.m.:

> The performing arts theater rented by the church is located on the corner of one of downtown Chicago's busiest streets. Once you enter into the doors you are met with dim lighting, low music, and a large bar 30 yards away with the alcohol visibly on display. If you failed to read the signs out front, welcoming you into a church service, you may have thought you walked into a lounge or happy hour spot. The lobby is filled with attractive, well-dressed young people. Most people are in groups in the lobby. One visitor that accompanied me said under his breath, "these people look like they are going for a night out, not going to church."
> —Field note

To capture the particular form of urban dweller the church covets, its leaders set up shop in an urban space recognizable to those familiar with the entertainment component of the city. From the lighting to the attire of those present in the lobby, members can embrace an ambiance that is consistent with a night out on the town.

Furthermore, young Chicago urbanites are situated in a city of entertainment. Chicago is known for its concerts, musicals, performances, and festivals held in iconic venues all over the city. In keeping with this theme, Downtown Church uses its rented theater space to capitalize on that entertainment orientation. Beyond the lighting, music, and bar in the lobby, the theater space allows the church to metaphorically transport congregants to an *event*. Its ambiance and rituals of preparation before worship are more suggestive of a "show" than a traditional Sunday morning service, expanding the nocturnal experience to a religious setting.

Bibles and Bars

Admittedly, the building lobby is a grand sight. The bar, which takes up almost the entire back wall of the lobby, is an old wooden bar, reminiscent of one from an old Chicago speakeasy. It gives the lobby a relaxed yet somewhat elegant, feeling. The pronounced presence of the bar often throws newcomers for a loop. I often overheard comments of confusion as to whether drinks were going to be served before service. It was not uncommon to see volunteer staff going behind the bar to play bartender, serving themselves or their friends a soft drink from the dispenser on the sly. I asked Davis, a Filipino band member, his thoughts about the bar as he helped himself to the soft drink dispensers.

> You know, it threw me off at first, but I think it actually works in our favor. People see it and I think they relax. They see we are not so uptight like other churches.

Davis, a Chicago resident for the past five years, clearly sees the bar as advantageous for the church. The bar area offsets any stigma that might be associated with the idea that church services are uptight and stuffy; rather, it allows potential members and established congregants to let their hair down. Not only does it provide a more appealing setting for their target demographic, but Davis believes the bar gives DC a competitive edge over other churches.

> Other churches are uptight, don't know how to have fun, can't relate to a younger crowd who likes to have fun, get dressed up and go out, enjoy a couple of drinks with friends.

Another member, an African American woman named Crystal, recalls her first impressions of the church upon attending her first service:

> I went inside and there's a bar. I was like, wow, can I order a drink and sit down, you know? It seemed like a club atmosphere, you know?

Crystal went on to explain that the presence of the bar offers her a sense of relief and relaxation, similar to the sentiments shared by Davis. She reflected,

> I didn't feel like the church was trying to make people hide the fact that they liked to go out and have a good time but instead embrace a younger lifestyle.

There is clear evidence that Downtown Church has had some success in translating the attraction of a nightlife atmosphere to the aura of the congregation. In that way, it is an important part of the church's quest for authenticity as a place for hip urban dwellers to worship.

We should note that the presence of the alcohol was explained as a consequence of renting out this particular space. A volunteer leader said that some Sundays they have time and can remove liquor before the worship service, but other times there is a matinee performance at the theater, which does not leave enough time to remove all of the alcohol from view. This explanation seemed odd, however. If the church is comfortable with the association with nightlife, and considering the *Absolute Church* ad campaign, why would they want to hide the alcohol? If Downtown Church is so committed to being different, why bother to explain away one of the primary ways it is in fact different? Why all the effort to explain why liquor was or wasn't visible week after week?

In fact, Barron regularly came early to help set up for the weekly service. The presence of the bar and alcohol seemed to coincide with marketing schemes that were part of the larger branding campaign for the church. During setup before one service, she asked Clairissa, a biracial woman who was one of the first members of Downtown Church, what she thought of the church's location. She replied,

> People don't know what it is. 'Cause they see a bar, some people think, well they call themselves Christians but they're not really. Or that it could be cult-like, or just the exact opposite. Because most people associate with a church being a physical structure versus a body of people with a certain spirit over it. And I think when you have a bar even though you're not selling alcohol, when you have a bar, um, in which alcohol is visible and with Buddha sittin' on top. I forgot about that. Have you noticed there is a Buddha sittin' on the bar? There are like 6 Buddhas all over the place in there so that also can send a very confusing message.

Marketing to the city isn't a clear, straightforward practice with a single set of signals. Clairissa's observations introduce the idea that not all patrons consume all aspects of urban areas, or religious spaces, in the same way. For some, the sacred and the profane are mutually exclusive and for others, there is more flexibility. The interface between the innovatively sacred and the impermissibly secular is consistently being tested for churchgoers in this unusual religious environment. What seems consistent is the extent to which this boundary negotiation relies upon images, discourses, and symbols that treat a white middle-class, materially oriented, entertainment ethos as normative.

After one evening service, I walked to the bus stop with Traynise, a 23-year-old, black college student from Michigan. We came upon advertisements for Smirnoff Vodka that were plastered over an entire wall of the bus stop. This prompted me to ask Traynise if she had seen any advertisements from the church. Tray said,

> Oh the advertisements? The advertisements on the trains and the buses, they didn't make sense to me. Some of it didn't make sense. Like, "Absolute Church" and you know when they put church signs on the purses and

shoes and I'm like, I don't understand . . . Like is that what's important to you or is that just to get our attention?

Traynise wasn't alone in her opinions. Dallas, a 20-year-old, white musician living not too far from the theater, told me in an interview:

I wasn't really sure what they were trying to say. It seemed like they were trying really hard to get our attention. And it doesn't really scream "church," you know? I wasn't sure of the message behind it.

While these representation schemes fall outside of the conventions of more traditional religious institutions, they reflect the distinct complexities found in a congregation where *location* is at the center of the church's identity formation schemes. Where other churches might place a denominational or a theological identity, Downtown Church elects to highlight the sensory experiences of city life. Through various advertising techniques and location selection, Downtown Church attempts to create a convincing city identity that would be considered authentic by those who understand the city as a place for consumption, entertainment, and social diversity. To the extent that these are the characteristics of the young, upwardly mobile city dweller, the church could well be attractive. These schemes are memorable and clearly piqued a sort of interest in these members, for better or worse.

There is the old adage that first impressions are everything. To make a big splash in the city and stand out from other churches in what is a competitive religious market, Downtown Church opts to take their cue from the consumerist aspect of the city, attempting to sell an experience and heighten the senses of a social class that resonates with these images:

I get it, they want to appeal to a younger crowd, you know so they put up stuff about shoes and drinks and handbags and what not. But I get it; they are trying and honestly, look around. I mean it's all young people in here so I guess whatever they are doing is working, right?
—Vance, black congregant

Likewise, Layla, a Latina member of the church and a recent volunteer, stated:

Like, so I think that from them [church leaders] they felt that they could be those young people to break that taboo . . . to break that stigma, and to just you know, let 'em know like, yeah, I'm young but I'm hip. I love God. I love people. And you don't have to sacrifice a fun-filled life.

The symbols displayed are not arbitrary, but are used to allude to an experience that brings together the church and the city in ways that coincide with popular patterns of consuming urban space. Even the timing of the weekly service is strategic. An evening service gives congregants enough time to sleep off their previous night's "nocturnal experience," if necessary. Congregants don't have to choose between enjoying a night out and waking up early for church. They can go out, sleep in, and continue their nocturnal experience in church that evening. Further, the evening service doesn't compete directly with Sunday morning services, allowing people to sample Downtown Church without having to abandon a previous church home.

Faithful Beauty

Retail and entertainment businesses that make urban nightlife a cultural "scene" regularly ensure that service personnel conform to dominant norms of feminine beauty, masculinity, and sexual allure. Leaders at Downtown Church enact similar strategies for their pastoral and volunteer staff. The displays of masculinity and femininity seen at Downtown Church reveal a certain hybridity—on one hand there are obvious displays of conservative notions of gender roles, at the same time there is significant reference to the sensual culture of urban nightlife. The pastoral staff has a keen interest in the appearance of people in positions where they might "represent" the congregation. This includes attention to body weight, height, modes of dress, hair, and the race and gender of the leaders and volunteer staff. Devotion to the aesthetic development of church personnel is a key tool used to authenticate the church as an attractive place to attend church in the city. In the racialized urban imaginary of church leaders, beautiful bodies help to sell downtown areas, whether it is for nightclubs, restaurants, or even Downtown Church.

The pastor just started implementing leadership meetings before the service, at 5:00 p.m. It is about 4:50 p.m. and leaders and volunteers are

standing on the stage waiting for the meeting to begin. There are about 34 leaders and volunteers present. The group is racially diverse, although all of the volunteer team leaders and pastoral staff are white. Most of the singers and musicians stand together while most of the greeters sit on the side of the stage. The room is filled with perfectly crafted smiles, thin physiques, and fashionable clothing. It almost feels like a casting call for a runway show. The majority of the women in the room are thin, wearing heels of some sort, in fitted clothing, and wearing makeup. Most of the men are tall, physically fit, and well dressed. It is about 5:00 p.m. now and the pastor's wife gets on the microphone and asks everyone to sit down. As she passes out the list of the order of service, one of the vocalists notices that her name is not on the list. She leans over to another vocalist and I hear her say, "I wasn't dressed to sing tonight so I'm off the list."
—Field note

All of the leaders who serve in visible positions (e.g., vocalists, greeters, musicians) during the weekly service are hand selected by the congregational leadership and are typically attractive, physically fit, young, and fashionably dressed. All those in visible volunteer positions are given a strict "style code" for their service. Women are given a small packet outlining acceptable styles of clothing to be worn during the service. However, it is not a packet outlining "modest" clothing but rather outlines current fashion trends from popular magazines such as *Elle*, *Glamour*, and *Vogue*. There is a certain ironic juxtaposition here—so many religious groups have made news for their dress codes that are meant to resist worldly fashions, and to hide potential female sexuality. Downtown Church does the opposite, embracing this aspect of "the world."

I sat down with Katrina at her home one Sunday afternoon before the service for an interview. She is a young black woman who grew up in various Christian denominations. Among other topics, the interview landed on the subject of the attire worn by some of the men and women at the church. Katrina recounted her experiences with the style code. As she spoke she showed me what she has kept from the packet. It includes pages with pictures downloaded from magazines and fashion websites, to give the women ideas as to what to wear that is current and fashion forward:

When I came I was handed these sheets of paper. I was on the worship team, playing the piano at the time. And the pictures were of women in different styles of clothes, you know real fashionable, like Emily [pastor's wife] and Linda [white woman who leads the children's ministry]. There were some cute styles but I thought, how expensive is this going to be, you know [laughter]? And I didn't think they were appropriate for church. Some of the stuff on there and some of the clothes some of the other girls wear, I think it's too revealing. I was taught modesty and so I always try to make sure things are covered or layered up so things aren't too tight. But it's different here. It is more about style and looking cute, you know, makeup and hair and high heels. I had to learn all of that or else my piano time will be cut short [laughs].

Katrina explained that she stopped serving on the worship team for a variety of reasons, one of which was the maintenance of her appearance. She found the fashion advice countered what she had grown up understanding as appropriate to wear in a church environment. Katrina mentioned later that even if her sensibilities were in sync with these styles, financially it would be too difficult to keep up with the requirements.

Each week the pastoral staff sits down and discusses who will make the cut to be seen on Sunday evening. This pressure often results in volunteers, and the paid staff, altering their appearance. Melanie, a black vocalist, began wearing a weave in her hair more regularly to achieve the desirable hair length she perceived was appropriate to fit in:

All the other girls just looked so pretty with their nice long, flowy hair. So I put my hair in so I could be cute, too [laughter].

Melanie wanted to fit in with the "pretty girls," the other female vocalists (who were white) on the worship team. Vanessa, a Latina volunteer with naturally curly hair, began to straighten her hair as soon as she became involved in leadership. But Vanessa laughingly laments that she can never get it as straight as Linda's, the white leader of her volunteer team. Deeply set in these style codes are Euro-dominated standards of beauty, and the women of color feel pressured, even if not always explicitly, to try to achieve them as they attempt to fit in and be one of the "pretty girls." Within the style guide, the examples of desirable beauty products, hair, eye color, and body types are heavily geared toward narrow conceptions of a Eurocentric beauty aesthetic. Melanie and Vanessa have internalized the implicit racial undertones of the physical expectations put forward and enforced by the leadership. As church leaders and congregants negotiate between their imagined ideas of what a church in the city should look like, we see how these imaginaries inform actual behaviors and organizational practices within the congregation across racial and gendered lines.

"Find a Hot Wife"

The emphasis on particular manifestations of physical appearance and beauty—and a significant and explicit attempt to use those standards to attract congregants—recently roiled the church. In 2007, Downtown Church released a YouTube video entitled "Find a Hot Wife." The video featured Randal, a member of the pastoral staff, energetically explaining to viewers that most churches "suck," but not Downtown Church where the pastor has a "hot wife" and "if you come to Downtown Church, you can find a hot wife, too." Images of Emily, the pastor's wife, came in and out of the promotional video. Emily is a former beauty pageant contestant and an aspiring model. She is often referred to by congregants and staff as a "life-size Barbie doll"—with fair skin enhanced by tanning treatments, long, platinum blonde hair, and bright blue eyes, along with a tall, thin frame adorned in sparkling jewelry, form-fitting clothing, and high heels. In appearance, she embodies white, heteronormative, feminine sexuality. Emily is often the center of discussion when she enters the lobby; it isn't unusual for members and church staff alike to wait in anticipation of what outfit she will wear that Sunday. Even the pastor's father regularly comments on her looks when he comes to the church. On a recent visit, while commanding the microphone before the congregation, the pastor's father said in an almost gloating tone:

> My daughter-in-law is so gorgeous and I know my son is extremely happy he has such a good-looking wife.

In this context, it is perhaps less surprising that church leaders would think it appropriate to feature Emily, and the theme of finding a "hot wife," in their video. In the video, Emily strikes different poses with different facial expressions—some pensive, some playful—with her blond hair blowing in the wind and her figure on display.

Church leaders anticipated that this marketing tactic would draw interest among young adults as they imagined young urbanites to consistently be on the hunt for the hottest mate (Grazian 2007). However, the advertisement video did not go over well. After multiple complaints from members and ridicule from bloggers all over the web, Downtown Church removed it. I first viewed the site a year after the video was pulled; however, a tech-savvy member was able to recover it and share it with me. Despite the video being pulled so long ago, the controversy surrounding it is still fresh in the minds of some of the members. Vanessa recounted how she felt when she saw the video for the first time.

> I couldn't believe they had that [video] up. It was so embarrassing. It's like hello, we [women] go here too. How do you think that makes us feel?

Through the expression of concern about its questionable taste, Vanessa continued and pointed out that the marketing pitch was directed toward heterosexual men, almost exclusively. There is no statement about finding a hot husband, or whether there might be a reason for people (especially women) of average physical attractiveness to attend. The video put forth a strictly heterosexual construction of sex appeal, with stereotypically European American representation as the standard of beauty. In the video Emily is on display for her prototype "hotness": blond hair, blue eyes, thin body, large breasts, and feminine dress. Women who fall into this standard are the desirable women, the hot women who are acceptable to become wives. And they are purportedly members of Downtown Church. Importantly, while the explicit selling of sex appeal may be surprising as a marketing tool for a religious congregation, nothing in the appeal itself undermines a conventional gender order in which men are the central actors and acquire attractive women as an important marker of social status.

Despite pulling the video in response to controversy, some in church leadership were a bit confused as to why it didn't go over so well. Pastor Paul said in an interview:

> I mean it was funny, you know we are in the city you know, clubs and everybody wants to go out and meet somebody hot and Emily is hot. People just took it the wrong way.

Pastor Paul's sentiments reveal the way the leadership imagines the city. In the racialized urban imaginary of the pastoral staff, the city is a place for entertainment, nightlife, and the prowl and hustle for romance. The city seems completely identified with sex and expressions of sexuality in Pastor Paul's comment, as if this flamboyance is a natural part of what comprises the urban. Moreover, there is a Eurocentric model of beauty at the pinnacle of aesthetic standards—and the pastoral staff finds that unproblematic as an imaginary for orienting the church's marketing strategies. The congregation, in this view, should be a part of this scene, not challenging it as (depending on your cultural politics) overly hedonistic, materialistic, sexist, sexual, superficial, or objectifying. Grazian (2007) explains that as the downtown urban nightlife scene has shifted more toward entertainment centers as the economic engines for cities, they have become sexual marketplaces. Masculine practices toward the sexual objectification of women are displayed in collective rituals that make public places like nightclubs and bars facilities for reproducing structures of gender inequality. Although Grazian notes that women ultimately have the final say in responding to the sexual advances made toward them, they are still objectified and commodified in this sexually aggressive environment. Downtown Church offers no critique of this urban reality.

Men are not exempt from the appearance standards that inform the congregation's marketing and self-branding strategies. One interaction demonstrated that the pressure is not always solely implicit. I sat with one of the members after a Sunday evening service. James is a short, black man with a light complexion and an inviting smile. He is always fashionably dressed. He had been a sort of staple in the lobby as a greeter for about four months, welcoming members, getting them involved in small groups, helping visitors meet others, and so on. But during the prior three weeks, he had not been out in front greeting. He had been doing more of the setup and tear down—a position of low visibility. I waited for him that evening after the lobby cleared out and helped him tear down some of the tables. When asked why he hadn't been greeting recently, he said the pastor had asked him to step down. Travis, a much taller black man and working model, replaced him. James assumed his displacement was because his look fell outside the constructs of desirable masculinity. So he spoke up. He told me that he had shared his concerns with the head pastor about the way the leadership teams looked, claiming that it misrepresented who is in the city of Chicago. He went on to say:

> I think that ties into the presentation of the church, definitely stylistically, and that is from clothing, weight, and just overall look, like one step down from sex sells. Where you know pretty people attract other pretty people and you know pretty people are good for the face of a business. But this is a church and so I think it [the marketing] gets all mixed up.

James's claim is that the leadership uses attractive people to get potential members interested in attending. The necessity of physical appearance in the overall authentication process communicates an assumption by Downtown Church that young adults are accustomed to a particular aesthetic in an urban space (Grazian 2007; Marti 2005). And, like any business, the face of those in front reflects those whom they are trying to attract. Height, weight, and clothing are all important to Downtown Church leaders, who strategically use members they think will be effective in bringing in the type of members they desire. James explained that the pastor was not receptive to his concerns, brushing off his comments and reassuring him that Travis had the "best look" for the greet staff.

Downtown Church leaders engage their racialized urban imaginary to construct an aesthetic that fits what is thought to be authentically "urban"—built on entertainment, consumption, and one version of ethnic diversity, but this vision is not altogether native to the city of Chicago. There is no guarantee that when you arrive you are "authentically Chicago" simply because you live in the city. In keeping with the fabrication of the urban authentic, even members are subject to re-branding. The racialized urban imaginaries of both congregants and church leaders are not static but dynamic frameworks that both challenge and influence each other. Voluntary organizations are in a market-driven environment in which they compete for the time and energy of potential members who can, in turn, expand their organizational resources (see Finke and Stark 1992). Downtown Church capitalizes on its volunteer and leadership staff to aid in manufacturing an authentic urban experience for their target consumers. In this case, a myriad of statuses and identities intersect to shape the experiences of current and potential congregants along gendered lines. The racialized urban imaginary of congregants and leaders continues to construct particular social locations regarding the urban dwellers within the congregation.

Class, Apple, and the Outside

Lights are always dimmed during Downtown Church's Sunday evening services, yet many of the faces of congregants are illuminated by the glow of smart phones throughout the service. Some use Bible apps while others take notes on their phones. The pastor and his pastoral team have conceptualized their congregants, not unreasonably, as members of the tech-savvy information age. Popular products like the iPhone, MacBook, BlackBerry, or iPads are consistently used, and often referenced, throughout sermons, marketing campaigns, outreach programs, and weekly church events. It is not uncommon to see the majority of the congregation on their BlackBerrys or iPhones during the services. Some, of course, are just texting, tweeting, or checking their Facebook status during the service. But the technology is also thoroughly integrated into the formal parts of the worship service and the congregational culture.

Pastor Phil usually preaches from his MacBook laptop and gears many of his messages toward the latest iPhone application or other social networking apps such as Twitter or Facebook. Many of the congregants respond favorably to the themes of the sermons and the use of social media. During an interview after one service, new member Stacey said,

> I like that he references apps [smart phone applications] that I use in my daily life. I can get it, which makes it easy to follow.

For Stacey, a member who had not previously been involved in a church, Pastor Phil's social media tactics achieve their purpose in engaging those unfamiliar with traditional sermonizing and Christian themed topics. Downtown Church as a congregation mirrors what is secularly available, adapting popular forms of entertainment and the cultural vernacular to compete in the secular marketplace for the devotion of its members (Flory and Miller 2008).

In fact, during numerous services, the pastor has discussed something "Apple" specific. He has stated during sermons that iPhones are superior to any other phone and "feels bad for anyone who is on team BlackBerry." The leadership staff and volunteers alike must be well versed in the tech consumption patterns of the aspiring consumer class. Concomitantly, congregants must also be well versed and have access to leisure consumption if they are to feel comfortable and included. The city of Chicago is not only hyper-segregated by race but is stratified by socioeconomic status. Making distinctive references to particular products that are affordable only to those in a specific income bracket can create a sense of inclusion or isolation, depending on which side of the coin you are on.

The technological hierarchy evident throughout sermons, like the marketing campaign focusing on designer church or acquiring a hot wife, facilitates a set of values that is concerned with the acquisition of material goods, technological competency, and a desire to stay on trend with all the latest in popular culture and media. To some extent, those whom the pastoral staff desires to fill their seats are mirror images of themselves—white, middle-class consumers of the city, attuned to popular culture and contemporary fashion imagined as essential to take part in the urban experience.

Implicit in the way the church regards the city and its racialized urban imaginary is the assumption of social class. As consumers of the city themselves, the church pastoral staff is actively involved in the culinary and entertainment scene of Chicago's weekend nightlife. It is not uncommon to see members of the pastoral staff and selected members of the volunteer teams leave together after the service to go out to eat, grab drinks at a lounge, or catch a movie. This is often a way to move up in the ranks of the church, and volunteers must be able to consume the city in the same way as their suburban-based pastoral staff. Unfortunately for those with less disposable income, becoming a volunteer leader can be costly. If one is not able to purchase the clothing, or pay for the dining experiences or movie tickets in the same way as those who drive in for a weekly visit, they are often etched out. Clearly this emphasis on leisure-based consumption has a hefty price tag and weighs heavily on those who can't afford to be a part of the church in the way church leaders imagine.

It was not uncommon for congregants to refer to the church as a business in their interviews, again, perhaps revealing the class base of the congregation. They perceive the sermons, advertisements, and the positioning of various people in leadership as part of a grand marketing scheme to draw in certain types of people. It is also true that congregants often express frustration and confusion with these tactics, as they believe the marketing communicates a very narrow understanding of the racial and class diversity within the city of Chicago.

> Well [long pause] I guess, well it's kind of like in the presentation of everything and then the word that goes forth, kind of comes with an expectation that you have experienced certain things that people in that socioeconomic group have experienced and then if you haven't you are out of the loop. You are kind of not in what is going on.
> —James, black congregant

James speaks to those who are on the margins. Those who do not possess the financial means to consume the city in a particular way may find Downtown Church an alienating environment.

Zukin (1993, 2004) argues that the construction of a city produces sites of entitlement and exclusion. For Downtown Church, the emphasis on a tier of class consumption, a nocturnal experience, and the aesthetic of its volunteers produces similar intersecting sites of exclusion that are implicit in the construction and development of its organization. Inevitably, when you craft an organization to target a specific group, the infrastructure is not made to handle everyone. A common theme in the culture of contemporary American Protestantism is that churches invite those wanting to worship to "come just as you are." But that ethos is not part of the congregational convention in every institution, and it does not seem to be a message coming from Downtown Church. The niche

marketing promoted by Downtown Church, and the dress and deport-
ment modeled by the leadership and expected of volunteer staff, instead
exude a sense of privilege for those who fit the image and exclusion for
those who cannot.

Consuming the City, Consuming the Church

Downtown Church's thematic worldview showcases how cultural values and religious identity are deeply embedded in the structures of
class, gender, and race, especially when embodied in an urban location.
Through various media and advertising techniques, church leaders hope
to gain members and increase visibility and recognition in what is to
them a relatively unknown environment. At the core of the stylistic elements of Downtown Church is a matrix of middle-class consumption
where material goods, aesthetically appealing people, and urban space
all intersect. The effectiveness of the matrix depends upon the success
in fabricating both this image of urban excitement and the congregation
as an authentic expression of it. Downtown Church uses innovative and
at times controversial tactics to adapt to the larger cultural trends they
imagine to be central to the life of a young person living in Chicago.
Varied modifications of traditional worship practices, molded to current
popular trends, speak to the congregation's dual need for authentication
as an "urban" organization and a competitive organizational edge over
other congregations in their market. Downtown Church leaders and
congregants negotiate between their imagined idea of what a church in
the city should look like and the structures of inclusion and exclusion
these imaginaries create. There are three ways in particular in which the
racialized urban imaginary of leaders and congregants informs organizational branding and shapes individual behaviors as the church seeks
to become a church for the city.

Selling the Urban Experience

Selling an urban church to prospective young urbanites in part requires
selling the urban experience overall. By focusing on how cultural producers, such as the leaders of Downtown Church, manufacture and
promote authenticity through high-end consumption and co-opting

elements of the urban nightlife scene, we uncover classed and gendered assumptions of the city and its inhabitants. Intersectionality works in tandem with the racialized urban imaginary to inform congregational discourse around the "ideal type" of church for the city. In the age of consumption, cultural distribution through symbols, perceptions, and branding is a key component in the consumption of urban space (Greenberg 2008; Zukin 1995). Downtown Church navigates through these cultural cues in order to understand how to "consume the city" and in turn produce its own "cultural object"—the congregation—to be consumed by others. Featuring images with cocktails, expensive handbags, and theater lounges dramatizes a given social status category, which may be as aspirational as it is reflective of members' current situations, but in either case clearly communicates an identity in which consumption is assumed. Downtown Church is not just a church service, it seems to say, but an overall experience. The weekly service creates a new place suspended between church and city. Its venue allows the congregation to identify as an authentic consumer and producer of urban culture in hopes of appealing to a young adult population reportedly on the fringe of religious commitment.

In *Branding New York*, Greenberg (2008) documents the cultural engine in New York that began to tap into the strategy of image marketing in order to appeal to potential visitors, investors, and residents on a cultural level. Greenberg introduces the idea of the psychographic technique, selling the experience and image of a place in ways that give it greater value even if it abstracts from the direct lived experience. Downtown Church's practices work to gain members by posing itself as a part of the "city," selling experiences and images in similar ways.

Landscapes of Privilege

Zukin (1993) describes landscapes as representing the architecture of social class, gender, and race relations impressed by powerful institutions. Landscapes such as the downtown area of a city embody these intersecting characteristics. Place entrepreneurs create and manipulate symbolic language to tell the public who belongs in the city and how to consume it (Zukin 2004; Mele 2000). DC leaders use similar tactics to attract their membership. We have seen how Downtown

Church interprets the culture of a public place like the city of Chicago and produces and advertises its congregation as consistent with that vision—even as an important part of achieving that vision or lifestyle. Members negotiate and often adjust to this projected image of the city. The multiple layering of imaginaries that construct Downtown Church, some of which are in conflict with each other, displays how assumptions, unintended consequences, and unexamined imaginaries (and privilege) end up shaping the congregation into a strange mélange of ideas and practices. Specifically, church leaders are intent on making sure their volunteer staff, most of whom are Chicago residents, are up to date on the latest technology, pop culture, and fashion trends. Hand-selected leadership and volunteers facilitate the strategic placement of aesthetically pleasing individuals in highly visible positions—and not just any pretty face, but faces that coincide with the expectation of urban space as conceptualized by the racialized urban imaginary of the middle-class white consumer (Lloyd 2006; Grazian 2004). The notion of "sex sells" is not a new concept for downtown establishments and is quite lucrative. Downtown Church incorporates its own version to capitalize on these conceptual frameworks in wooing the target demographic.

The collective engineering of a religiously infused nightlife experienced by church leaders and volunteers favors heteronormative Eurocentric standards of beauty, those with the purchasing power to consume the city in very specific ways, and those with the cultural capital to successfully maneuver in this highly classed environment. Successful involvement in the congregation requires the accomplishment of a related set of styles, gestures, and behaviors by congregants and volunteers. Those who fail in those efforts, or who have imaginaries about what an urban church should be that conflict with those of the church leadership, are eventually phased out of volunteer opportunities, and in some cases, from a sense of inclusion in the congregation.

Seductive Salvation

Many city centers in the United States are experiencing a "re-population"—often with single young adults or with retired empty nesters. This demographic shift helped to produce a surge of churches catering to these populations. The congregations often interact with urban environments in new and innovative ways. Downtown Church, as one example, has latched onto the urban nightlife scene as a means to connect to its desired demographic. Previous research has found that when developing a new congregation, members embody the cultural and religious values they cherish. Thus, these emerging institutions give those values and traditions a place to thrive (Chaves 2004). Congregations also express a sense of identity and value (Edwards 2008; Becker 1998). As we saw earlier, Marti (2005) argues that individuals are more likely to become part of a congregation if they make a connection between the congregation and some element of their person. Thus, as social life evolves, and new social arrangements arise, churches begin to adapt to emerging cultural trends in an effort to continue to provide an attractive place for individuals and communities to worship (Flory and Miller 2008; Chaves 2004). The members' collective identity evolves as the organizational culture adapts to them and vice versa. In the case of DC, promoting the consumption of a nocturnal experience creates a sort of collective interaction which reproduces social inequality on the basis of gender as displayed by church advertisements and dress codes. Traditional notions of masculinity and femininity supported by church leaders and congregants alike reflect social hierarchies at the intersection of race, class, and gender that work to create the social locations of groups within the congregation. Of course, congregants who are sufficiently wary of the tactics may willfully ignore or maintain a sense of skepticism in order to enjoy the service or engage in the congregation, but there may be limits to the positions of authority within the organization that they can achieve.

Downtown Church is an unusual and perhaps even unique place in which elements of city life and imagined city life come together. The nuances of these conflicting worldviews display how cultural values are deeply embedded in the intersecting identities of race, class, and gender, especially when embodied in an urban location. There is the underlying assumption that the best of those in the city are attractive, have particular consumption patterns, and are from, or will be from, a particular class standing that affords them the ability to consume in a specific way. Volunteer leaders and other members of the congregation are concerned that the organizational structure of the church sends out conflicting messages regarding who the church is for and how they go about attracting this target demographic. At the same time, the different orientations and expectations urban dwellers bring each Sunday evening do allow for complex exchanges within the congregation. Downtown Church is selling a complex bundle of goods in a competitive religious market. And it is in this way that the racialized urban imaginary is enacted by both congregants and church leaders in ways that create spaces of exclusion and inclusion for those willing to consume this form of congregational body.

As church leaders and congregants explore the boundaries of a consumption-oriented ideology of what makes the city exciting, they also pursue a model of racialized authenticity that assumes ethno-racial diversity as constitutive of urban Chicago. Next we turn to an exploration of these models and how they work with the consumer orientations to shape how the church understands religion in the city.

3

The Diversity List

I mean we are in the city so I kind of expected it [the church]
to be diverse.
—Ben, white congregant

I think that ties into the presentation of the church where
aside from the leadership only being white, those who are
under the leadership or are in main key roles, have to look a
certain way as well, definitely stylistically . . . ethnically that
is where they provide their leeway to seem diverse.
James, black congregant

Part of the current allure of downtown areas is their transformation
from an industrial to a cultural location where middle-class consumers
can come to encounter diversity—as experience, as entertainment, as a
part of personal identity. In this way, diversity becomes an object to be
packaged, marketed, and consumed, marking the "authentic" aspects of
the urban experience available for middle-class patrons. Racial diversity
in particular is a highly anticipated component of this project. Encoun-
tering the racial *other* downtown becomes a part of a racially charged
consumption centered on the racialization of the urban landscape.

As we have seen, Downtown Church attempts to portray a particular
type of "urban" image in order to attract a particular type of urban consumer as member. The mix of young, up-and-coming urbanites, drawn
to the consumption of designer goods, with aesthetically pleasing and
unconventional environments, informs much of the image-marketing
and organizational practices of the church. Involved in this conceptualization is the precarious presence of racial and ethnic minorities
within the congregation. This chapter turns the lens inward to focus on
organizational practices that shape interracial interactions within the
congregation. These interactions uncover various orientations to con-

gregational diversity, and the attendant fears, goals, and racial experiences surrounding the presence of certain minority groups within the congregation. Implicit in these conceptualizations is the intersection of class, gender, and a racialized consumption among a congregation pursuing an urban religious identity. These varied social locations intersect within the spatial context of the church in ways that shape the racial experiences among congregants and expectations of diversity within this urban congregation.

Imagined Diversity

In the racialized urban imaginary of church leaders and congregants, racial diversity is just as common to the city as its skyscrapers. A downtown location effortlessly affords them the racial diversity that is imagined as organic to the urban environment. Many newcomers to the church are quickly drawn to the visible presence of members from various minority groups within the congregation, signaling a familiar and expected component of the urban environment. At first glance, there are the faces of people of color and white folks in the lobby, on stage, in the weekly announcements, and among the congregants. Ask any congregant and they are likely to describe their congregation this way:

> We have Brazilian, Korean, Chinese, and I think Pastor Chuck's family is from Lithuania.
> —Katrina, black congregant

> I would describe our congregation as culturally diverse, we have people from everywhere.
> —Joshua, white volunteer

> Yeah, the first thing I noticed here was all of the diversity here. When you walk in there are all types of people in the same place.
> —Vanessa, Latina volunteer

Yet not once during the weekly service, in programs, in leadership and board meetings, or on the website, is racial diversity ever mentioned—as a goal or as a social process. Church leaders do not concern themselves publicly with cultivating a racially diverse membership base or inclusive rituals. Church leaders believe racial diversity will naturally present itself to the church:

> If you want all-white congregations, go to the suburbs. But if you are in the city, you should expect your church to be diverse. That's just what the city is. That's what the city does.
> —Pastor Craig

Despite this seemingly casual air about it, racial diversity is a selling feature for the church. Racial diversity signals to the urban consumer that Downtown Church can extend the authentic urban experience to the religious setting. Pastor Paul explained,

> Diversity is already built into the city so people expect it wherever they go. If they are at the movies, shopping, walking downtown, they just expect it. So if you have a church here and you don't have it [diversity] at your church, then you are doing something wrong. If people want to come to a church in the city they are expecting to see that and we have that here. It's something we can show them, like see, we are diverse.

Pastor Craig and Pastor Paul thoroughly "place" diversity, that is, they associate it with location—the suburbs or the city—as if the connection were natural and even logical. Just like "downtown" is fun and exciting, it is diverse with multiple options in both activities and people. Pastor Paul makes the connection clear, in that his claim that non-diverse congregations in the city must be doing something wrong follows immediately after noting the many shopping or entertainment options downtown. Consumer culture and social diversity are intimately and seemingly inseparably connected. This assumed naturalness of place, and the ways in which diversity is almost natural, exists even as Downtown Church recognizes the necessity of marketing the congregation in a competitive religious setting where potential congregants are more or less literally "church shopping."

Despite these claims to the importance and authenticity of diversity, there is still some ambivalence by church leaders toward cultivating a racially diverse congregation. At the core of their racialized urban imaginary is the presence of the African American community. Recall the declaration by church leaders that Downtown Church was not a "black church." Their fear of a racialized corporate identity is linked to the disproportionate number of black Americans inhabiting urban communities, and has a profound effect on the ways in which they understand their organizational identity as a *downtown* church. However, church leaders do not altogether resist an African American presence in their congregation. They imagine black folks, urban blackness, and genres identified with African American expressive culture and style to be a fixture in the city of Chicago—an expected component of the "authentic" urban experience. Thus, much of the racial politics within the congregation are affected by a negotiation and appropriation of urban blackness by church leaders and often a complicity in this appropriation by congregants.

Managed Diversity

Throughout my time at the church I observed an organizational practice we identify as *managed diversity*, in which church officials strategically manage the visibility of black volunteers, appropriate elements of urban blackness, and yet studiously avoid racialized cultural texts and religious practices within their congregation. The management of diversity legitimates the congregation as not being "too white" but rather a diverse, authentic urban establishment that is appropriate for young, hip urban dwellers to enjoy. This profile provides a competitive edge over nearby churches vying for members in the same location and among the same target demographic. At the same time, the church leadership controls the number and visibility of black bodies in order to prevent the perception of a black organizational identity. Linked to the management of diversity are the gendered and classed expectations of those who are consuming and those who are being consumed. Managed diversity is a set of techniques organizational leaders employ to align their vision of the church with their understandings of "the city." Church officials implicitly build on the historic relationship between black Americans and the urban environment to market their congregation. In turn, their management of diversity has divergent effects on the experiences of their congregants.

Blackness and the Urban Cool

During the weekly services it is not uncommon for Pastor Phil to reference famous black rap moguls, celebrities, athletes, or issues in the hip-hop world in the hope that such references connect him to his hip, urban membership base. During a sermon one Sunday, Pastor Phil opened up the service by holding up his iPhone and asking,

> Do you guys follow Diddy [black rap mogul] on Twitter? [Silence] He has really inspirational things to say. He grew up in a city not too different than Chicago. The man is so cool, if only I could be as cool as him. Everyone should follow Diddy. He's such a huge success.

Pastor Phil also attempts to facilitate a *call and response* component to his preaching, a staple in traditionally black congregations. He will give instructions to the largely white membership complete with the appropriate "response," which is often a concoction of hip-hop slang and traditional black preaching styles awkwardly rolled into one:

> Can I get some help with the word? It's ok if you say "preach, preacher" or "holla at ya, boy" to let me know you are feelin' what I am sayin'.

While this specific kind of call and response (spoken in an affectation of a "black" vernacular) is characteristic in traditionally African American churches, Downtown Church leaders are adamant that they do not want to be recognized as a "black church." Rather, Pastor Phil co-opts certain elements of black church culture or celebrity that he deems as advantageous in appealing to his audience. Some members let out a chuckle, others clap, yet it is rare that he receives any of the responses he requests. Black members throughout the congregation almost never respond and in some cases are confused by his efforts:

> I'm sitting next to two black members, Erika and Lacy. They are both Chicago natives and grew up on the Southside. During the service Pastor Phil kept on saying, "it's alright to talk back to me during the service. You can say 'holla at ya boy' or 'preach'. I'm alright with that." As he was giving these examples he added his impression of a "black" dialect. Oddly

enough, most of the people sitting in the audience are white. Erika and Lacy are stoic during his impressions. Erika began to shake her head and let out a deep breath as Pastor Phil called for more responses throughout the sermon. Lacy's leg began to shake quickly every time he would start in his black dialect. I approached Erika after the service. When I asked her why she was shaking her head she said, "I mean, I just don't like it when he [Pastor Phil] does that, you know tries to talk black one week, then act like he knows what's up the next. It's like he is trying so hard 'cause we are in the city."

—Field notes

Diversity from the vantage point of the white consumer motivates the pastoral staff to participate in the appropriation of black entertainment and religious culture as a means to provide their target demographic with an authentic urban church experience. However, the efforts fall flat for some members who are black, or reside in the city, or both, rather than consume it as a distinct and partitioned experience.

Black Men and Urban Authenticity

The appropriation of urban blackness is not restricted to the service but, as we have seen, is reinforced by the strategic placement of black bodies in visible positions throughout the lobby and the church service. For leaders of Downtown Church, their success in the urban religious market weighs heavily on their ability to attract the young urban consumer through the commodification of urban blackness (Grazian 2004; Johnson 2003; hooks 1993). However, the leadership staff is not completely alone in this expectation. When congregants describe their first impression of the congregation, they almost always reference the "diversity" of the membership as a defining feature. Routinely, their descriptions narrow in on the African American volunteer staff:

JOSHUA (WHITE MEMBER): I would describe us as diverse. When I first got here, Larry (black man) and Travis (black man) greeted me and we have been cool ever since. There is so much diversity here.

RACHEL (LATINA MEMBER): The church has a real multicultural vibe, we have women from Brazil, and international students who

come in and out and then I mean look around, we have Brian and
Melanie on stage (black singers), Monty and Nathan (black greeters)
greeting you. I mean diversity is all around.

Bell and Hartmann (2007) note that for Americans, race is at the core of
diversity talk, and implicit racial knowledge is almost always assumed.
Their observation certainly holds for Downtown Church congregants, as
diversity translates in part to the visible presence of African Americans
in the congregation.

While African Americans are one of the smallest groups at Downtown Church, the majority of black folks within the congregation have
volunteered at some point and most were positioned in visible volunteer
posts such as greeters, ushers, musicians, and singers. One particular
pattern jumped out at me during observations. Week after week, I noted
that black men were often asked to serve in greeter positions but white
men rarely are asked to do so. Some black men stated that they had no
intention of getting involved but the pastor said they had a "great look"
and could represent the church well. While this coaxing persuaded some
of the men to join, others were skeptical. Before an evening church service, one of the members scanned the lobby, pulled me aside and said:

> You know, it's like you walk in and see all of these brothas and you're like,
> whoa, wait a minute, what are they [Downtown Church] trying to do? You
> know they got Travis (black greeter) out there in the front then they got my
> man Rich (black greeter) over there working the table. It's like they are re-
> ally trying to say something, like yeah, we're in the city, we got some niggas.
> —Larry, black congregant

Larry, a personal trainer and Chicago native, came to Downtown
Church for a chance to help start a church and expand his business.
He met the pastor and his wife at the gym when they were in town on
a visit. When they told Larry about their plans to start the church, Phil
and Emily personally invited Larry to get involved. Yet, as time went on,
Larry became acutely aware of the utility of the church's black volunteer staff. He acknowledges this interpretation of the urban context as
a racialized and gendered representation to legitimate their presence in
this space (Grazian 2004).

As previously noted, Downtown Church leaders are very particular about the type of person they place in visible positions to represent the congregation. For instance, the male black greeters were typically tall, physically fit men whose tastes, speech, and dress coincide with the upwardly mobile young adults the church is trying to attract. These men assert a type of urban masculinity in their physical appearance and deep skin tones that is alluring yet safe enough to experience for the middle-class consumer (Johnson 2003; hooks 1993; Childs 2009; Russell-Brown 2008; Grazian 2004).

> After the leadership meeting was over, Pastor Phil stopped Travis [black greeter] at the door and then turned to me and said, "You know, it's like when Travis started standing out front for us. We started getting a lot more strong black women to come here and get involved, and men like him, too. He has been a nice addition."
> —Field note

Pastor Phil made this statement with a big smile as he patted Travis on the back and then walked down the hall. Travis looked at me with a smirk, shook his head, and left in the opposite direction. The pastor is not shy about his tactics and is open about their perceived benefits, but Travis seemed both dismayed and dismissive of his role. Travis's presence is used as bait to attract, "strong black women . . . and men like him, too." And who are the men like him? I observed the continued use of four specific black men as greeters who were tall, physically attractive (one a Calvin Klein model, another, a personal trainer), and typically involved in the nightlife scene in the city (two were well-known DJs and club promoters) or well-educated and well-networked in the community. These men are not representative of African American men in the city of Chicago; rather, they represent a version of urban blackness that can reinforce the safe, authentic "downtown" experience church leaders are hoping to cultivate.

The idea of the "strong black women" Travis is on task to attract aligns with a long-standing stereotype attributed to black women as independent, lacking the need or desire for assistance, and often implicitly noting the absence of desirable feminine characteristics (Collins 1999; Durr and Wingfield 2011). Perhaps coincidentally, Pastor Phil rarely spends time interacting with black women who volunteer in the same way he does with the black men. Yet, there is one black woman who serves as an elder at the church and another black woman who had a short appointment as the administrative assistant to the pastor. In interviews, both women expressed a "lack of direction and attention" from the pastor. These women, along with other black women who volunteer, are often described as "strong go-getters" by the pastoral staff. But this seemingly translates into little attention from the pastor regarding their leadership positions or the expectations for their volunteer roles. Black women are rarely appointed to positions of high visibility and spend less time in their volunteer positions than black men. Capturing and appropriating urban blackness is thus at times gendered, allowing black men heightened visibility with the pastor and at public worship. This affords black men interactions with church leadership that are not available in the same way for black women.

Pastor Phil never gives examples of black women in his sermons in the same way that he does for black men. Many white suburbanites are increasingly listening to rap and hip-hop music, and spending much time watching professional sports and becoming fascinated with the gendered images they represent (Rodriquez 2006). This may allow black men in a majority non-black context to gain status. In contrast, black women do not have the same kinds of cultural signals to trade on for status and visibility. Granted, African American men must contend with stereotypes that paint them as violent and aggressive. However, through the management of diversity, the pastoral staff curtails negative racial associations by strategically placing men they deem "a nice addition" in places where they enhance the urban experience the church is cultivating.

Importantly, some of the men stated that they were interested in leadership within the church, but their current volunteer position was not what they had in mind. Larry stated:

> It's like Michigan Avenue . . . you [black men] can buy but you can't own, it's the same thing here at Downtown Church.

Larry acknowledged that the church is a mirror image of the dominant culture in which society resists integrating black men into positions of power, influence, or leadership (Royster 2003; Collins 1997) even if they are celebrated in other ways or for their talents.

At Downtown Church, non-black volunteers are often propelled into volunteer or leadership positions of influence and authority; this hasn't happened for black men. Some volunteers in higher-tier positions describe their journey to the top as an expedited one:

> I was really nervous . . . well, I am still really nervous that someone is going to come up to me and ask me something and I won't know the answer. I don't even know the books [of the Bible], can you believe it? I haven't even been to a Christian church before this one. But about a month after I started coming, Phil asked if I wanted to help and so I help to co-run the children's ministry.
> —Vanessa, Latina volunteer

Similarly, a member witnessed a comparable experience for another volunteer:

> You know girl, it's crazy. I see people like Chad [white man in charge of the worship band] and I think, "wow, he just got here and he is already running the show." It's like they just threw him in there so fast. I don't really think he is ready and he seems overwhelmed but they really like him. He hasn't even been here that long.
> —Leslie, black vocalist

Unlike others, black men participate but are not elevated into upper-tier positions. In her study of multiracial congregations, Edwards (2008) found that a congregation was open to hiring a black pastor as long as it did not have any major impact on the church or worship styles. Once a black identity becomes too prevalent, the idea of having a black person in more prominent or authoritative positions becomes less attractive to white (and sometimes minority) parishioners.

An interview with Chad (the music director referenced in the quote above) revealed that he had never led a worship team prior to coming to this church. The music component to the service is one of the most important components to an evangelical worship service (Chaves 2004; Marti 2012; Dougherty and Huyser 2008). Styles of worship, song selection, and music type communicate not only a particular religious and organizational identity but a racial one as well (e.g., Gospel music is associated with black congregations). Chad, knowing the importance of the worship team, expressed reservations about taking this role so quickly and even stated at times that he would like to share the responsibility with a more experienced member. However, the pastoral staff encouraged him to take on this position and ensured that they would be there to guide his musical selection.

Competitive Diversity

Have you visited those other churches around here, you know like Central? They are so boring. They are basically all white, not for me. They're not like us.
—Chad, white music director

The vast majority of evangelical congregations remain racially segregated, even those that have made concerted efforts to pursue racial diversity within their churches. As Emerson and Smith (2000) and others have noted, Evangelical Protestantism has some built-in tensions regarding race. This is particularly true regarding evangelicalism's focus on the "individual" as the site of faith, renewal, and social change. The emphasis on individuals is anticipated to lead to a welcoming attitude and acceptance that transcends racial and other barriers; at the same time, it can result in an intended or unintended blindness to social structures that are racially built. Evangelical congregations struggle in varying degrees with this discrepancy, but most are keenly aware of the issue and at least in theory want to transcend the racial division within American society, or at least within the church itself (Wadsworth 2014). Therefore, the racial utility of specific minority bodies in Downtown Church offers the congregation a competitive edge over neighboring, predominantly white, churches in the Chicago area that have "failed" in this pursuit of racial diversity. The quote that begins this section calls attention to the ways in which church leadership (in this case Chad, the music director) is attentive to this dynamic with Downtown Church. Indeed, responses from church members, but particularly from church leaders, consistently reference DC's diversity as a clear distinction from other congregations and an advantage that makes it a better option for those looking for an authentic urban church.

Having a select number of non-white members, and displaying their bodies in particularly visible ways, appeals to and aligns with the expectation of racial diversity in the city as anticipated by the racialized urban imaginary. Churches in urban spaces face an open market in terms of attracting members (McRoberts 2003; Martinez and Dougherty 2013), and all congregational actions must be regarded in that light. One member noted how this works even in the generally controlled staging of the church's public presence:

> I think that ties into the presentation of the church where aside from the leadership only being white, those who are under the leadership or are in main key roles, have to look a certain way as well . . . definitely stylistically . . . ethnically that is where they provide their leeway to seem diverse.
> —James, black congregant

The concern with competitiveness in the local religious market, even when not articulated in those terms, emerges time and again in discussions about what makes Downtown Church special, the need to attract a particular type of member and how that is done, and why DC is authentic. The concern is understandable among the pastoral leadership, but as we see, it permeates into the membership when it comes to the congregation's diversity.

Whatever the claims to the benefits of diversity, however, the church leadership is overwhelmingly white and the dominant worship style comes out of the white Protestant Evangelical tradition. After one of the evening services, Barron assisted Melanie, a black vocalist on the worship team, in taking down some of the sound equipment. She began to discuss her disappointment with the music selections:

> I mean we are in Chicago. There are so many types of people here . . . [whispering] . . . I keep asking the pastor about changing up the music to represent all of the people here but I get nothing. I have asked three times and he doesn't change anything. I mean why not be proud of what you have and represent the people here? I mean why can't we have a little salsa, Latin, gospel . . . something?

For many multiracial congregations or those attempting integration, the music selection is assumed to weigh heavily on the success of their endeavors (Ammerman 1997; Becker 1999; Christerson, Edwards, and Emerson 2005; Edwards 2008; Marti 2005, 2012). Members view an integration of culturally distinct rituals and worship practices as a sign of respect and inclusion for non-white members in these traditionally white spaces (Marti 2012). Yet there is no diversity in the genre of music (e.g., songs in Spanish, Gospel music) or programming events offered by Downtown Church. Despite the lack of integrative worship services, Melanie stated that she would continue in hopes of convincing the pastor to reconsider the music selection.

While many people spoke of the importance of diversity in their motivations for being at Downtown Church, others shared a more skeptical view of how genuine it is, and saw it as too tied to issues of competition. Linda, a white volunteer leader, lamented in her interview,

> Diversity is just a token value here. It is something that the pastor uses to one-up the other churches in the area . . . that's all it is.

Indeed, during fieldwork at Downtown Church, there was not one sermon, distribution of religious materials, or staff meeting dedicated specifically to racial reconciliation, multiculturalism, or integration. If diversity was to happen, it was to be without the focused nurturance of the church leadership. The church leadership is concerned with creating a space the young urbanite can consume. In the racialized urban imaginary of the white pastoral staff, racial diversity is implicitly often a performance for prospective middle-class consumers in the market for a "less white" religious experience. This leaves integrative rituals beyond the scope of the organizational goals.

Image Control

Tensions did arise, however, and were often fraught with racial implications, subtexts, and occasional explicitness. For example, I was invited to a meeting convened to address a confrontation between the pastor and Crystal. The meeting was in response to an e-mail Crystal wrote stating her concern about the lack of ethnic, racial, or cultural integration in the music selections. Pastor Phil never responded to her e-mail, which resulted in a heated confrontation between the two in the lobby right after a Sunday evening service. The pastor claimed that he thought the e-mail was from another Crystal in the congregation. To rectify his lack of response, he wanted to hold a meeting regarding the music and asked me to join.

The meeting opened awkwardly. I sat squished in-between Crystal and her best friend on a small love seat while the pastor sat directly in front of us with a coffee table in between. The two members of the band, a white man and a Filipino man, sat on the couch right next to us. Pastor Phil starts laughing to himself, stands up, and then begins to tell us a story of his recent visit to an all-black congregation in the South,

> "There were all these old black women and they had brooms. Then they started shooing and sweeping the devil away. It was so retarded. They looked so retarded (laughter). I never want to be that traditional. It was so retarded."

My informants squeezed my hand every time Pastor Phil laughed. He continued to laugh and make fun of these women for five long minutes. After he realized no one in the room was laughing, he quickly switched the subject to the worship styles. He stated that he was interested in having more "hip-hop and urban styles" in the service, as was suggested in Crystal's letter. Crystal began to get excited, never bringing up her disappointments with how the pastor "straight up disrespected" her by never responding to her e-mail. Instead she began to spew out ideas about having turntables in the lobby, hosting a spoken word night and on and on and on with ideas. Pastor Phil nodded with a smile as everyone began to give ideas about adding rap and a DJ to the service. And just as the excitement began to build, Pastor Phil shot down the ideas.

> "Well, Chad, when you guys tried something new it sounded like crap and I don't want that to happen again. I want to make sure everything we do up there is perfect. I think we should stick to what we have now because it sounds good and everyone loves Hillsong [a white, contemporary Christian group]."

Everyone quickly got quiet. We all realized at that moment that Pastor Phil had no intention of changing anything. Pastor Phil excused all of us and asked Chad to stay so he could go over song selections. We left quietly.

Crystal stopped attending Downtown Church shortly after the meeting. She was hurt and thought the pastor had made a mockery of her suggestions, of black religious traditions, and had lumped all black religious expressions together. For our analysis, however, Pastor Phil's actions and words in the meetings were enormously revealing, if complex to understand. First is the straight-up contradiction of professing to want more "hip-hop" and "urban" features in the worship service and then instructing Chad to stay with the Hillsong repertoire. Second was the incredible tone-deafness (as a most generous interpretation) to others' sensibilities in openly mocking something he observed in a black church when the room had three African American women present and the meeting was called specifically because one of the members was upset that her suggestions to integrate the worship service had been ignored. Third was yet another expression of the fear the Downtown Church leadership had of being labeled a "black church" and thus how much of the church's expressive culture and public presence had to be monitored. And finally, there was the claim that "everyone loves Hillsong," with no recognition of the cultural origins of the music and the racial identifications connected to those origins.

However, it is not just inclusive styles of worship that can be on the chopping block at Downtown Church. Visible blackness is not always a highlighted feature, either, even if African Americans are often put in positions as greeters. As we have seen, associate pastor Paul conveyed that the leadership team was cautious about any of the volunteer teams appearing to be "too black." He stated that the pastors have even removed some of the black volunteers from their leadership positions and placed them in other positions in order to change a team's appearance. When asked for an example, he immediately replied,

> So it's like in our children's ministry, we had a conversation like, why are all of the teachers black and you're [team leader] the only white person?

He went on to say this conversation resulted in the relocation of some of the black women to other volunteer teams. These adjustments were made regardless of ministry preference or the experience of the black volunteers. Notably, church leaders were not concerned with the children's ministry appearing "too white" or overrepresented by any of the other groups present in the congregation.

When I asked Paul to elaborate on this process, Paul focused on the music selections during the Sunday service:

> You have to make sure the culture isn't shifting one way or the other—so it's like a lot of times we get pounded by some of the team some of the, I don't know what the right terms are, some of the black people on our team, pounded, why don't you do more gospel music? Well a lot of things we do already appeal to the African American culture and if we did gospel too it would create a shift that might—'cause you know a lot of white people like the music and a lot of black people like this. 'Cause a lot of people would argue, why wouldn't it go that way, those are the people who want to come. 'Cause diversity is a part of our core values and in order to be truly diverse you have to manage it.

Although an assistant pastor, Paul struggles to find what he views as the "correct" terms to use to refer to the black membership base. Clearly, a familiarity with the dynamics of racial labeling is not a qualification for joining the leadership, nor does there appear to be any training regarding dealing with diverse groups around such issues. More importantly for our analysis, he expresses a clear understanding of the potential for a larger black presence in the congregation, and the leadership's concern about that potential. For Paul, an uncontrolled amount of "diversity"— for example, the presence of too many black individuals on one team or too much music associated with the black church—will cause the infrastructure to change. In order to be truly diverse, Paul states you must manage the visibility of black volunteers, the number of black members that you attract, and the amount of inclusive religious practices offered.

Race-less Diversity

Despite the centrality of diversity to Downtown Church, with some members citing it as a motive for attending and Associate Pastor Paul describing it as a "core value," interviews revealed that both white members and members of color often stressed that they were relieved by the lack of "race-talk" when they first began to attend Downtown Church. Members discussed the church as a sort of "race-less" racially diverse space where race was not the main focal point. Natalia stated:

> I mean it was really cool when I walked in, you know all different kinds of people and race was never mentioned which was a breath of fresh air. But now it's just strange that nothing is ever said about it. Usually churches would jump at the chance to talk about it.

Natalia assumed that the church is an inclusive space where no formal recognition has to be made. However, over time respondents once in support of a race-less space began to view the congregation as untapped potential to cultivate a multiracial religio-culture.

In a race-less space, racial sensitivity in congregational programming is often overlooked. The concern with "not shifting [the culture] one way or the other" keeps the church in the default mode of white evangelical music and worship styles. Consequently, organizational programming is marked by the racialized urban imaginary of white church leaders shaping the overall experiences of members along racial lines. In the effort to constantly provide new and innovative ways to communicate the gospel, these types of oversights can be costly.

Night at the Movies

It wasn't uncommon for church leaders to create innovative and interesting components to their Sunday services. A "Night at the Movies" is one way they used to bring the parables of the Bible to life. By using a truncated version of modern films intertwined with mini-sermonettes, Downtown Church leaders create a movie-going experience complete with interpretive messages in place of a traditional Sunday service. One night *Antwone Fischer* was the feature film. The film tracked the real life story of a black man who was beaten and molested as a foster child, and through his membership in the armed forces found the strength to reconnect with his birth mother and extended family. Throughout the movie the N-word was used constantly. For this screening it was not bleeped out, nor was there any disclaimer or warning by the pastor at the beginning of the film. Further, there was no time for discussion or processing of the experience—of the film or the use of the racially derogatory language—at the end. But every time the word was uttered there were visible or verbal responses from members. Some shook their heads, others had their hands over their ears, some closed their eyes and looked away. Still, in every scene the pastors selected to show, the N-word was used repeatedly. And with every utterance, it cut many parishioners like a knife. Indeed, the gasps or movements throughout the congregation, occurring repeatedly, happened even though the majority of the people sitting in the audience that evening were white. The scenes contained images of black women on welfare, women addicted to drugs, violent black men, and abusive black households—a gamut of images that, while perhaps true in this individual case, also reflect negative racial stereotypes aggressively associated with the black community at large. But Pastor Phil never addressed the racial implications of the film. He only addressed Antwone as an "individual" in his sermonettes throughout the film. Once the film ended, the lights came up and Pastor Phil encouraged everyone to get some popcorn on the way out. After the service, I tracked down Jayce, a black woman and member of the church. She was visibly disturbed during the film, holding her hands over her mouth and closing her eyes when the N-word was repeatedly used:

> I mean really? You are just going to have a movie with the N-word flying around like that? I know there are only a couple of us [black people] in the crowd but damn! That was totally inappropriate. People see these images and think that is the case for all of us and not just an extreme case. Out of all of the movies out there, this is the one you pick?
> —Field note

In this space and event, black members experienced both hyper-exposure and invisibility. In selecting this movie, church leaders failed to understand the social context in which the movie was to be viewed and were silent about the large cultural themes in which the movie's messages resonated. A group of three men, two black and one white, were headed toward the popcorn machine and one of the black men said,

> Yo, did they really just have the N-word out there in the church like that?
> That was crazy, yo. They had a brotha feeling uncomfortable up in there.
> I wonder how the white people felt?

For black members, the movie reinforced negative and costly stereotypes about the black community. Furthermore, there was the emotional distress members experienced, caused by the constant use of the N-word throughout the film. Yet this was apparently unanticipated by the pastoral staff, unperceived by them as it was happening, and was certainly unaddressed in the collective setting.

Although racial epithets are unfortunately heard in many places in American society, in a religious setting such as a church service, they are unexpected. One black member came over to me smiling and said sarcastically,

> How did you like all those "nigger" references huh? That's always the way
> I like to start a church service.

Religious services are generally places where people feel welcomed or safe, but this evening was different. The movie selection heightened tensions and created distrust in the leadership staff. Members grappled with their confusion and speculation as to why that film was even shown. Black members felt invisible to the leadership with their film selection, and hyper-exposed because of the open images often used to condemn African Americans in US society. Some questioned whether they were truly welcomed in the church. Natalia asked,

> I mean how can they just do that as if we [black members] are not here?
> Did they even think about us? Probably not, they probably don't even
> care.

Significantly, some non-black members also expressed discomfort:

> That was heavy, dude. I'm not sure that was the best movie to show, especially with the N-word. That was kind of a lot.
> —Joshua, white congregant

That wasn't right. They shouldn't have done that. That was so uncomfortable. I can't imagine what black people in the audience were thinking. Like if I were them, I would be so uncomfortable, and mad. What were the pastors thinking?
—Jazelle, Latina congregant

For church leaders, racial diversity and inclusion take a color-blind or color-invisibility approach in which we are all "individuals" rather than recognizing how race is a central feature of everyday life. Diversity can be praised, even highlighted, and is regarded as the natural and welcome outcome of urban life. But it simultaneously seems to shut down serious attempts at discussing race, and racial advantage or disparities, and removes the need to be intentional about correcting past and present injustices. The color-blind approach can leave minority members disenfranchised, offended, and on the receiving end of being ignored, without the cultural resources to address that situation. Becker (1998) attributes the "problem of race" in building religious communities to racism, ignorance, intolerance, and unfamiliarity. Becker claims that the solution for these religious spaces is to become a discursive space where people can talk about their discomfort. For the members of Downtown Church, a discursive space is not provided. Conversely, Downtown Church communicates no ecclesial call to pursue racial diversity at any level within the organizational structure, leaving little room for discussion or accountability.

Night at the Movies is an attempt to break through traditional conventions and bring forth the message of the church in a new and innovative way. Church leaders play on the entertainment facet of the city, hoping to transform the evening service into a movie-going experience. However, the feature film, *Antwone Fischer*, reinforced notions that Downtown Church, like many evangelical churches, is a white institutional space in which the racial other becomes an afterthought in organizational programming. The film's selection sent conflicting messages of what is allowed, who belongs, and what is acceptable at Downtown Church.

Attraction and Disillusion

As we have seen, in the racialized urban imaginary of Downtown Church leaders, diversity is something to be consumed. Superficial efforts at inclusivity often fail to meet the needs of a racially diverse space, especially for those who cannot pretend to live in a race-less society. I met David at a casual eatery downtown. David is a physically fit black man and one of the first members of Downtown Church. After describing his first encounter with the pastor and his wife at the gym (similar to the way Larry met Phil and Emily), he started telling me about the church:

> DAVID: I saw a lot of diversity, just off of first judgment, but none of our first judgments are ever correct . . . a lot of things I wasn't really connecting with the church.
>
> BARRON: What were some of the things that you weren't connecting with?
>
> DAVID: The culture right away wasn't that new to me. But I wasn't really used to it. I had grown up around diversity but diversity here [the church] was . . . it seemed one-dimensional to me. But after going there for a few weeks or a few months I realized that the only reason it was one-dimensional was because it was a young church and it was still growing.
>
> BARRON: What was that dimension?
>
> DAVID: It seemed to me to be geared toward young white America, the music, the tone, a lot of the speakers were Caucasian and I wasn't seeing that diversity that was being talked about.
>
> BARRON: What type of diversity?
>
> DAVID: The racial diversity.
>
> BARRON: That was talked about in church?
>
> DAVID: Ummm . . . not at the church, I'm talking about in the Bible. Jesus had 12 disciples and they were all from different backgrounds, different beliefs . . . but I think to magnify anything you have to celebrate diversity. You're not going to draw people if you don't celebrate people and who they are.
>
> BARRON: Can you give me an example?
>
> DAVID: Well, I could tell when shaking a few hands and talking to a few people that a lot of people have never maybe saw a young man

like myself act like I act or carry myself how I carry myself, a young black man. In our race, there is a lack of black male leadership so most people see us as the jolly athlete and they put me in a box, and I don't like that, I took that personally. Most of America grew up on TV. This is what they see on TV, you all commit crimes, are great athletes, make funny jokes, and you can sing, rap, and dance. But you can only give what you know. So at church blacks are all in service positions. Having no blacks in leadership speaks a lot to what you are trying to do. If you think this is how you should do things, I am more worried than offended. You show me what you think when you do things. I don't have to ask you anything; all I have to do is look.

BARRON: What have you seen?

DAVID: I think everyone can walk through that door, but the offer isn't extended to everyone like it should be. I don't think a kid from Overland High (inner-city school on the West Side of Chicago) would be welcomed here. Let me put it to you this way, it's like me building a house in the middle of your house and telling you, you can't come in.

Many newcomers to the church are quickly drawn to the visible presence of various minority groups within the congregation. Upon first glance, there are all sorts of faces in the lobby, on stage, in the weekly announcements, and among the congregants. However, as weeks go by, congregants such as David begin to recognize that things aren't always as they seem, and others suggest that maybe diversity is only about the competitive edge, not principle. Instead of what he views as biblically based integration, David finds stereotypical views of black men, a lack of corporate integration, and racial barriers that make their "church for the city" less inviting to some.

Seasonal Diversity

Diversity as a consumable feature of an urban religious experience is not always sustainable. As an organization where racial diversity is treated primarily as either a marketing tool or a symbolic gesture by the leadership, it is not uncommon for Downtown Church to experience stretches of time where racial diversity is nearly non-existent. There are times when there is a larger racial minority presence in the church and other times when the attending congregation is nearly all white. Antoinette, one of the few black women in leadership, stated:

> Yeah for a while we had the "black corner" where Larry, Monty, Crystal, and some of the others would hang out. But after a while, most of them stopped coming. You know it will go in waves. Sometimes we have a lot of people of color and we are really bumpin' and then it just falls off.

Antoinette attributed these "seasons" to the "freshness" and "excitement" that Downtown Church presents to people who are from more traditional, mono-racial churches. But after a while, she claims "they get frustrated with the lack of inclusion in our services and they leave." There was a stretch of nearly two months where Larry and Travis did not attend. This left a large deficit as Larry did all of the video announcements and Travis was their prized greeter. Then one Sunday they reappeared. I rushed over to greet them and inquire where they had been:

LARRY: Ha, yeah you haven't seen me. I have been boycotting . . . (laughter) . . . Travis always boycottin'. You know black men on boy-cott. Sometimes you just need to leave to give them a wake-up call.

BARRON: What kind of wake-up call?

LARRY: You know. Wanted them to see what it was like without us. Wanted them to know that there are consequences to just having us around but not really making a place for us here. If they don't want to do it, then we don't have to stay. And for me, I had to reconnect, you know? I had to get right with myself so I wasn't participating in the petty behavior. You know, getting frustrated and doing or saying something that wasn't really me.

BARRON: What do you mean by petty behavior?

LARRY: I mean a lot of the issues here are about immature individu-als. You know, people here are young, trying to figure things out, so you're gonna run into people being ignorant about things or focus-ing on the wrong things. They got something going on here worth being a part of. When you can get young people, of all different races, in one place, in the city of Chicago, that's major and you know it. The church is everything we want it to be that we can't do at other churches or other places in the city.

Members constantly asked the pastoral staff where Travis was and said that they had missed his face greeting them in the lobby. However, the pastoral staff was unable to give any concrete answer as to why these men had left. Their absence without an explanation caused an uncomfortable stir in the congregation, leading to various narratives as to why these men would leave such high-profile positions. It provoked some members to revive the discussion of inclusive worship styles, while others decided to follow Larry's and Travis's lead and leave the church as well.

The "black boycott" wasn't at all unique to the black membership base. There were seasons when the Latinx presence in the congregation was low as well. When I inquired why these "diversity droughts" might occur, many members attributed the shifts to the lack of culturally representative worship styles, lack of recognition for racial history months, the token use of hip-hop, rap, and "urban" culture in sermons, and the overall apathy toward racial recognition in the congregation. Others chalked it up to the growing pains of a newly forming congregation whose leaders are not from the city. Whether this latter factor was related to the leadership's lack of understanding regarding certain racial matters, or whether it was just a matter of learning a new turf, was often not made explicit. Both possibilities, of course, are possible.

After one such diversity drought, I interviewed Sonja, a black woman and former volunteer, to understand why this occurred in the congregation:

BARRON: Who do you see on the fringes of the congregation?
SONJA: Well I would have to say right now (long pause) we don't have
    that many right now, we do well we have a few African Americans.
    The African American community, ummm, because we have not
    established that multicultural feel so much yet like in our music and
    things of that nature so I'm sure that it's probably—like worship and
    the music here is pretty caucasian-y. People who are used to different
    groups and different styles will probably go through a culture shock
    and I know many that feel disconnected.

After the interview, Sonja and I were leaving and unexpectedly ran into another member of the church. We began chatting and Sonja brought up her thoughts about some of the questions that had been posed in the interview. For the next 35 minutes, Sonja and the other woman talked about their dislike of the racial dynamics within the church, emphasizing the "segregated lobby," "white music," and the "black corner." We all laughed as they became very animated with their descriptions of how the church would be if they allowed more "black styles" of worship and more Latin drums in the band. "Only in a dream," they said, would their "rainbow church" be realized.

Larry's comments about coming back to the church, since it is "major" when you can get people of different races in the same place in Chicago, and these two women's enthusiasm for a true "rainbow church," indicate how seriously some of the African American members regard the promise of Downtown Church. Race isn't invisible to them, nor is it "merely" visible—they want a deep trans-racial congregation for religious and cultural reasons. These hopes are often frustrated by the shallow, laissez-faire approach to racial differences displayed publicly by the pastoral staff, especially combined with what seem to be deliberate back-stage efforts to keep the congregation within the control of the white staff. But the power of the hope keeps them returning to Downtown Church.

Consuming Diversity and the Power of Consumption

In an attempt to market a particular vision for young urban residents, church leaders end up producing "the city" as an object expressed and embodied in part by persons of color. Enmeshed in the racialized urban imaginary of church leaders and congregants are racialized, classed, and gendered understandings of the city of Chicago and, in turn, the utility function of race for a church in the city of Chicago. Racial diversity wears a variety of hats within the congregation and is defined in multiple ways by the congregants and church leaders. This results in experiences of both incorporation and exclusion for members. Specifically, the racialized urban imaginary produces assumptions within which the congregation exists, while managed diversity and racial utility work as the set of techniques employed to align the congregation with this vision of the church. It reveals clearly the connections between race, religion, and the city. These embedded processes create differing conceptualizations of diversity resulting in three key racial processes that are integral to organizational outcomes.

Power Structures of Consumption

First, part of the city's allure is the ability of the middle class to consume diversity as an experience, as entertainment, and in this case, as a part of a religious identity. Consuming diversity, in part, becomes an expression of class status and a certain cultural capital; it is chosen, fun, and comfortable. Downtown Church leaders themselves represent this social location as upwardly mobile, white men and women who cultivate urban tastes and aesthetics. They use their own *habitus* to influence the religious preferences, practices, and affiliations of their congregation as a young, hip, but "not black" church for Chicago's young urban adult. But simultaneously, church leaders create the congregation as a "safe" place to consume racial diversity as an extension of the urban experience. It doesn't threaten a color-blind approach to race, nor disrupt fundamental distributions of power. Diversity becomes an object with instrumental value for church leaders in that it may help them gain congregants. Church leaders and congregants imagine the city as fundamentally marked by diversity, and that diversity has a necessary racialized component. In particular, black bodies within the congregation become objects to be consumed, to be enjoyed, but not to be identified with or adopted. Church leaders preserve a subject-object distance that makes the Magnificent Mile and the management of diversity in the church two similar experiences.

Thus, it seems that the relationship between race and place, in conjunction with the need to establish an urban identity, drives Downtown Church to participate in racially charged practices influenced by the racialization of the urban landscape. In *Blue Chicago*, Grazian (2004) presents an innovative analysis that captures the popularity of racially charged consumption as a component of the contemporary urban landscape. He observes that the disproportionate number of black Americans inhabiting urban communities has a profound effect on the ways in which some urban spaces are represented and consumed. A consequence of the overrepresentation of African Americans in poor urban communities results in black people becoming a fixture of urban America—an expected component of the "authentic" urban landscape. For Downtown Church, this structural reality translates into an expectation of the presence of black people in urban environments and in turn an expectation of a black presence in the congregation. Attached to this expectation is the idea of authenticity.

A major organizational practice employed by white church leaders to develop their ideal congregation is what we identify as *managed diversity*—the hierarchical control of diversity that maintains its usefulness to the goals of the organization but keeps it from threatening either internal church authority or the external religious identity of the church. This managed diversity has produced complex and consequential outcomes for racial experiences within the congregation.

Intersectionality helps to explain how gendered and classed dimensions of a racialized identity operate differently across racial groups, based on the consumption of diversity in an urban space. Black men, in particular, embody a form of symbolic capital in urban spaces and are therefore a prime focus for the church leadership. Not all forms of black masculinity are prized, however. A particular form of black urban masculinity becomes a success as a consumable aspect of diversity. Black men who served as volunteers display an upwardly mobile status, which requires the accomplishment of a set of related styles, gestures, vernacular, and behaviors considered culturally appropriate to the "downtown vibe" church leaders are trying to cultivate. Black women, and other racial groups, do not seem to offer the same level of consumable capital that is offered by the presence of black men in this specific spatial context. In the racialized urban imaginary, there appears to be a *hierarchy of racial diversity* as a result of this particular interpretation of intersecting identities in the downtown urban space. Ironically, black men are at the top of this hierarchy, which results in them being a particular focus of management. Ultimately this hierarchy shapes the experiences of black men, women, and non-black members in complex ways. The racial utility of black men results in an overrepresentation in second-tier leadership positions of high visibility, but a lack of opportunities to move up in the ranks as do many other non-black volunteers. As scholars have previously reported, black members are often marginalized in multiracial congregations (Edwards 2008; Emerson and Woo 2006; Marti 2005). At Downtown Church, their marginalization is distinct, given how the church leaders interpret their presence in the city.

Representations shape our perceptions of the world, others, and ourselves. The predominantly white church leadership staff is in charge of the images that are put forth for public consumption. Through the racialized urban imaginary of the creators of Downtown Church, whiteness and middle-class tastes are directly connected to their interpretation of the city, its culture, and manipulation of its symbols. The differing class and racial cultures of the consumer and the consumed within the same congregation allows social class and racial status to condition the religious organization of Downtown Church as well as the conceptualization of specific groups within the congregation.

Divided by Diversity

In the second form of racial process, the conception of racial diversity, and the practices of managed diversity, complicate members' capacity to become integrated into the organizational community. Previous research on multiracial congregations claims that multiracial networks are equitable exchanges between white and non-white members (Emerson and Yancey 2008; Hunt and Hunt 2001). Multiracial spaces can also support minorities in transcending their racial identity in order to become a part of the larger spiritual community (Marti 2008, 2009). However, at Downtown Church, many of the volunteers understand the usefulness of black bodies for church leaders seeking to promote the congregation, creating a dynamic in which racial and ethnic transcendence is much less likely. Conversely, Downtown Church communicates no ecclesial call to pursue racial diversity in their services, materials, or leadership meetings, leaving little room for discussion or accountability. As we have seen, Becker (1998) attributes the "problem of race" in building religious communities to the lack of a discursive space where people can talk about their discomfort. For the members of Downtown Church, a discursive space is not provided. Instead, discussions of race are suppressed by the visible representation of its black members and a focus on individuals within a default white Protestant religious culture. It is often noted that when a church is confronted with infrastructural changes centered on the incorporation of culturally distinctive styles of worship, congregations become resistant (Ammerman 1997; Becker 1998, 1999). This notion is consistent with Edwards's conclusion that "Interracial churches remain racially integrated to the extent that they are first comfortable places for Whites to attend" (2008:6). The pastoral staff of Downtown Church is adamant that they do not want their church to "go that way" or become a "black church." Therefore, they are fairly inflexible about their stance that the congregation's religious practices and rituals mirror the preferences of the white pastoral staff—implicitly privileging whiteness and white normative styles of worship.

Furthermore, when integrating racial minorities into predominantly white spaces, racial diversity does not often affect the core culture and practices of these organizations (Berrey 2011; Bell and Hartmann 2007; Collins 2011; Edwards 2008). Instead, racial diversity is often treated as an addendum to the overarching organizational structure and is sparingly addressed (Marti 2012; Marvasti and McKinney 2011). As Marti (2012) discusses the relationship between music and race in the church setting, he asks whether diverse music can be the gateway to facilitating a racially diverse congregation. In the reverse, one could ask, is the resistance or refusal to incorporate racially associated styles of worship music an indicator of a church's stance on racial integration? Like other organizations, many evangelical congregations remain structurally ambivalent about the process of integration and therefore are less successful in achieving racial diversity beyond visual representation (Collins 2011; Edwards 2008; Marvasti and McKinney 2011).

Church and City

Third, it is essential to recognize the duality present in the conceptualization of the church in the city. For church leaders, there are perceived benefits and consequences to the presence of specific groups within the congregation based on their conceptions of the city. Pastor Paul and the leadership team are careful that the racial and class aesthetic they are promoting communicates the appropriate identity the church is establishing. Managing diversity is a way to manage the delicate balance between a *downtown church* and *inner city church, black church,* and *"not too white" church.* The racial context of the urban landscape, coupled with a classed expectation of their target demographic, leads to the practices of placing the *appropriate* black members in visible positions. But this strategy works against any attempt to move the church beyond this place in order to focus on cultivating a racially inclusive space for its membership. In a competitive organizational environment, the racial utility of black representation appears to offer the church the ability to outbid its neighbors vying for the same location and target demographic. The pastors anticipate the visibility of black members as a way to communicate success in navigating the city's racial landscape, which implicitly and sometimes explicitly is meant to communicate failure on the part of their predominantly white counterparts. However, this focus on competition comes at a cost to members seeking more racially inclusive environments.

External structural forces coupled with cultural imaginings of the urban landscape influence racial experiences within Downtown Church. Various patrons discussed their particular expectations of how racial diversity should operate in their congregation; moreover, a distinct expectation seemed to emerge from the church leadership's actions. In focusing on the various forms of racial diversity within the congregation, we are able to understand how the racialized urban imaginary that has been so prevalent in white Protestant thought, and is brought together and intertwined with a consumption approach to experience with a particular generation and class, results in a congregation that simultaneously wants diversity, keeps it managed and at a distance, and uses it to market itself. The varied and complex understandings of racial diversity come as a response to the racialization of the urban landscape, the complexity of race in America, and the embeddedness of religion in the racial order. These cultural practices display how cultural values and religious identity are deeply entrenched in the structures of race, especially when embodied in an urban location.

These complexities are not confined to the four walls of the church but are expanded as the church seeks to become an active part of the Chicago political landscape. We now turn to the outreach ministries focusing on the involvement of volunteers and church leaders in endeavors that engender more substantive social contact with structural and systemic inequalities throughout the city. As Downtown Church engages in a form of racially charged production of religious identities and consumption of diversity as a value, these worldviews shape organizational practices and interactions beyond Sunday services.

4

City Outreach

But you know Phil likes all these brothas out here playing on his team. It's like he's playing a pickup game in the
'hood—something he's always dreamed of (Shaun and
Larry begin to laugh so hard they almost choke on their
food). But this is also a good way for us to bond as men. It's
like we get to just be us, outside of church. You know we
cuss and get aggressive and competitive but it's all good. It's
a good way to bond. And it doesn't hurt to have the principal on our team this year since we are getting into the high
school now.
—Larry, black congregant, post–basketball game
conversation

It was a cold and icy evening in Chicago—just the perfect weather to
spend inside a muggy gym watching some competitive local basketball.
The men's community basketball league plays games on the border of
the West and South sides of Chicago, bringing in a diverse group of
competitors. When I walked into the gym, I was greeted with a blanket
of humidity, the sound of shoes squeaking on gym floors, and blowing whistles filling the air. Booming voices yelling, "Foul!" "Let's go!"
"Defense, Defense!" "Pass me the ball!" echo throughout the gym while
multiple games are played at once. Then I spotted them—Downtown
Church men's basketball team. Despite representing the church in the
community league, the team was never advertised at the church. I only
heard about the game through Larry, one of the respondents who plays
on the team. He invited me as he explained, "I figured you would want
to see this since you come to everything else we do."

In the gym the team is easy to spot. Their upscale black uniforms are
a far cry from the regular, league-issued jerseys of red, green, or blue
mesh that are worn by the other teams. The Downtown Church men

wear black jerseys and matching shorts, lined with red and yellow trim; they are complete with the church logo and number on the jersey front and the player's last name and number on the back. Downtown Church also has a very tall team of eight, appearing to be the tallest in the gym. As I scanned the team, however, I saw three people on the team I had never seen before at DC services or events. One is an older black gentleman, perhaps in his early sixties. He is athletic looking with white hair and a salt and pepper beard. The other two are black men in their early twenties, each standing about six feet four inches, with their athletically built bodies adorned with tattoos (I learned later that they are Shaun and Dre). The only white men on the team are Pastor Phil and his intern, Evan.

The game began; Downtown Church was playing an all-white team, many of whom were middle-aged. The game intensifies quickly. Shaun and Dre had a talent level that surpassed others on the court. Repeated fast breaks resulted in flashy dunks and trick shots. Other DC team members shared in the athleticism and talent on display. Watching them play against this competition was like watching an NBA team play a high school team. Not surprisingly, emotions began to run high as the trash talking and cursing between the teams heightened. The men on the opposing team were constantly yelling and complaining to the referees that the game was too physical. Pastor Phil was also frustrated, but for different reasons—he thought that the pace of the game was too slow. He yelled at Larry, who had been in the entire game, to hustle down the court.

The opposing team was having a hard time scoring, which only increased the tension and the intensity of the game. The referees repeatedly reminded the teams, "ease up guys, let's ease up." But team member Cole didn't heed their request. After a foul, Cole stood chest-to-chest with one of the men on the opposing team. After a few seconds of intense stares, Cole pushed the man in the chest. The man stumbled backward and the referee called a technical foul. Cole retreated to the bench, as the technical foul disqualified him for the rest of the game. The quarter finished and the buzzer sounded. Final score: Downtown Church wins, 70–41.

After the blowout, Downtown Church's team members huddled together. Pastor Phil scolded the men for not playing together as a team and not maintaining their intensity and focus. After the huddle, the team members dispersed and began to put on their coats and leave the gym. Larry and Shaun invited me to join some of the guys for dinner to brief me on what I just saw. As I walked toward them on the court, Pastor Phil intercepted my path and introduced me to the older man who was playing on the team. He is the principal of a public high school in the city, a school with which Downtown Church recently entered into a partnership for a volunteer program. He is a well-known figure in the community, and is said to be close to the local ward alderman and other prominent political figures in Chicago. After I shook the principal's hand, Pastor Phil began to talk with him as if I was no longer standing there. Phil told the principal why he couldn't attend any of the events at the high school, but assured him that there would be some grand events—substituting for the pastor's physical presence. The principal responded by telling Phil that he is a great organizer and the school is lucky to have him. The principal gave me a nod and walked off; Phil thanked me for supporting the team that night and left.

I caught up with Shaun and Larry, and they decided to go to a local diner a few blocks away from the gym. As they stepped out into the cold, Larry said to me,

> I saw you talking to the principal of Overland. Bet you were surprised to see him on our team. Yeah, Phil tried to get at me today, yelling at me like he's the coach or something. Get out of here, man, I run circles around you [laughs]. He [Phil] tries to weed me out like the token Negro, but the principal comes through me. He's [the principal] still not done feeling Phil out though."

The conversation picked up in this vein after we got seated in the diner and the food arrived. Larry continued his thoughts begun earlier about the high school principal's involvement on the basketball team. Although Larry claims the connection with the principal is his doing, he speculated that the pastor put the principal on the team as a strategic move to get in good with city officials and the alderman.

> Phil is trying to purchase a building in the city and you know how Chicago is, no one is making any moves unless you know someone. And since they're outsiders they need people to vouch for them. That's why

our team is so good and why our uniforms are so nice. He isn't going to ask the principal to be on our team if we not lookin' right!

Shaun chimed in,

When basketball season comes around, I get a phone call. That's why you really haven't seen me at the church. And you really don't see Dre [the other non-church member playing on the team]. They only call on us during the season 'cause they know we can play, and they want to be good. They are trying to make a name for themselves out here.

Working in the City

Outreach ministries to the surrounding community are a long-standing feature of evangelical churches. This extended vignette about DC's participation in the community basketball league offers a rich portrayal of a number of different dimensions of the ways in which the racialized urban imaginary informs Downtown Church's efforts at outreach into Chicago. Like all imaginaries, it informs the organizational planning of the church by influencing what people think is real, and thus what should be done and how it should be done. While church leaders and congregants engage this age-old evangelical practice of outreach ministry, they bring together varied orientations of what outreach ministry *should* look like and how they should go about it in the city of Chicago.

Participation in basketball leagues is a common characteristic of post–World War II American religion. It is notable that the Downtown Church team participates in a community league rather than a church league; as Shaun pointed out, the church is "trying to make a name for themselves" in the community, consistent with its efforts to reach previously unchurched or disaffected people. But it also reveals some of the tensions within Downtown Church regarding the racial utility of its black members—particularly black men—as a way of bolstering its credibility as an urban and diverse congregation that thrives on its location in a cosmopolitan city. Larry and Shaun laugh about Pastor Phil imagining himself as a city-bred basketball player, and call attention to what they see as a failure to truly reach out to those "who need God"—calling them only during basketball season. At the same time, they recognize the opportunities for community that the church and basketball team provide them.

The basketball league participation is also tied to a key outreach ministry that Downtown Church features in its printed materials and programs. Larry twice referred to connections to a high school in one of the roughest parts of Chicago, the West Side. Downtown Church had recently made an announcement during the Sunday service that the church would be running a volunteer program at the high school every week, staffed by church members; as noted, the principal of that high school is now a member of the DC basketball team. Larry saw these two occurrences as clearly connected. The high school volunteer program was significant in several ways, not least of which is that it was DC's first attempt at a continuing outreach program. But it also revealed the various ways in which DC consumes the city and grapples with—or fails to confront realistically—issues of race and class. Finally, these efforts together—the basketball team and the high school outreach—reveal another paradox. The church's organizational practices simultaneously led it into clumsy public postures, often involving cringe-worthy public statements from the pastoral staff, while nonetheless making it possible for some church members to do important work, both for themselves and for their community. Competing worldviews about the relationship between church and city reveal the complexities within Downtown Church's approach to outreach ministry that generated inclusion, exclusion, and opportunity in the city. They are essential to understanding why many parishioners stay with Downtown Church.

Church, Gender, and the Politics of Outreach

As noted, several of the men active in the church and on the team see the basketball team as serving a few distinct purposes. First, putting together an all-star roster of athletic men, along with fancy uniforms and an undefeated record, allows the church to stand out in this local basketball league. It is a form of advertising, in a sense, but advertising done in a particular venue with a particular cultural message—nothing says "urban" in contemporary American culture quite like basketball. Downtown Church officials may still be managing diversity but they are extending it beyond church walls, reaching out to others who may not be accessible through more traditional church circles. Simultaneously they are in a way using the racial utility technique to extend the church's brand.

At another level of community connection, the team may well provide a means for the church to broker relationships with city powers. According to Larry and Shaun, church officials not only want to make a name for themselves with their select target demographic, but they also gain social network connections and organizational credibility in the city's political arena. Downtown Church is somewhat successful in these endeavors, securing an outreach partnership with the local high school and having the school principal associated with their team.

Larry also points out that this team is a site for male bonding. As he indicated, the team play and the chance to be together outside of worship services clearly offer a time, place, and a means for community and solidarity among many of the men in the church, particularly the men of color who are at the center of the team. Those opportunities, in a work-centered urban environment in which people have many competing demands, should not be overlooked. This chance to socialize implicitly acknowledges that such bonding does not occur, or is more difficult, in church. However, on the court, Larry says the men can "just be us" rather than playing a circumscribed role at the church. On the court, Larry isn't a church greeter with official duties and thus caught in the web of social expectations, but is just "one of the guys." He finds this opportunity valuable amidst all of the wheeling and dealing going on around him. Shaun and Larry understand that this bonding is segmented, in part because Shaun (and Dre) are only called upon when basketball season rolls around. But they participate, and enjoy. As Downtown Church teeters between a consumption-based ideology and racialized authenticity model as ideals for realizing religion in the city, informal bonds prove to be harder to come by than might be expected. These men recognize a sense of freedom on the court that is not replicated at the church.

Interestingly, Larry and Shaun recognize that there may be an undertone of consumption by Pastor Phil, linked to their male bonding and to the competitive sports engagement. They claim, joking but quite in earnest, that being part of the team is a way to live out the urban fantasies of the pastor and his assistant—white men who live in the suburbs and would not otherwise have the opportunity to play on an all-black team in the city if they didn't organize one in their own church. The racialized urban imaginary becomes influential on the part of church leaders not only for personal gain but by using Larry, Shaun, Dre and others, in a way, as props in the construction of DC as an authentic urban church. But Larry and others in turn find space to accomplish some of their own goals, and to resist some of the organizational practices that institutionalize the leadership's race and class privilege.

Conversely, participation in the city league has opened up influential doors for the church, and is assumed to be a contributing factor in providing a chance to get a foothold in powerful political circles within the city. This seems to be what facilitated their first ongoing urban outreach ministry for Downtown Church, as the high school ministry is the church's first attempt at outreach on a consistent basis. They are committing to serve the students within the school weekly, and in that effort will face issues connected to residential segregation, poverty, neighborhood violence, education reform and resourcing, and race relations in the city, all on Chicago's notorious West Side.

"You Are the Light in a Dark Place": Overland High School

It's great you know? We have been able to adopt Overland High School. Do you know Overland has one of the worst attendance rates? Over 70% of the kids don't make it to their first class. We here at Downtown Church have the opportunity to adopt this high school and love on these kids and serve them.
—Pastor Phil, Sunday evening service

Using some of the connections made from the men's basketball league as well as the networks of black church members, Downtown Church "adopted" Overland High School, a public high school located on the West Side of Chicago. Overland struggles with violence, inadequate resources and facilities, and the challenges that come with a student body that is largely low-income. Overland has one of the lowest attendance and graduation rates in the city. The Downtown Church staff had never worked with a minority youth population or inner-city school programs; Pastor Phil appointed Linda, a white woman who had just completed an MA in human resources and secondary education, with an emphasis in multicultural curriculum development, to lead the effort. Volunteering for the outreach was open to all members of the church; however, fewer than a handful of members actually committed to the ministry.

Every Monday, volunteers from Downtown Church are to meet at the school at 7:00 a.m. to encourage students to get to first period. In showing up every Monday the pastoral staff hopes to start a type of "school club" atmosphere, such that students will feel a part of something and thus be more apt to get to school on time and go to class. The pastoral staff anticipated, or at least hoped, that the presence of church volunteers every Monday would create a school culture of punctuality and discipline. In meetings with the pastoral staff, and from the pulpit, Pastor Phil made it clear that he viewed the "problems of Overland" as directly tied to the individual efforts (or lack thereof) of the students. During a Sunday service, Pastor Phil brought up the church's charge to help these students:

> All these students need is a hug, and to know someone cares, and this will give them the motivation to get out of bed and get to school on time and be their best. If we are there when they get there, with a smile, we can set the example. With time and effort, we can help improve their attendance. We have a chance to change the culture at the school.

With this prompting, the pastoral staff decided to name this outreach ministry the *Breakfast Club*, presumably, but perhaps un-ironically, after the John Hughes movie about alienated middle-class white teenagers. For their inaugural meeting Pastor Phil and Associate Pastor Paul brought a catered hot breakfast, to be eaten by volunteers and the students. Chase, a volunteer, recounted the day:

> We didn't really know what we were going to expect. We weren't really told anything, just to show up and be at the school by 7 a.m. in this room. And then I walk in and there is all this food laid out. The spread was massive, with bacon, eggs, sausage, waffles, pancakes, muffins, coffee cakes, bagels, orange juice, and these Danishes with the jelly and icing on them. Phil and Paul were there. They were just kind of standing in the back, not

really interacting with the kids or us. They were kind of just observing. Like observing how we interact with these kids in "their natural habitat."

Keisha chimed in,

> He and another pastor came in and ordered this extravagant breakfast for all of the kids and then watched us interact. It was really awkward. The kids didn't really know what to do with it and then it set up that expectation every time and we sure as hell can't do that every Monday. And he [Pastor Phil] hasn't been back since and neither has that breakfast.

Travis followed up,

> It did make it a little awkward. The kids really didn't know what to do with this food. It wasn't what they were used to and they didn't know us so it was like the food was the elephant in the room. Everyone was a little uncomfortable, trying to feel each other out and then here is all this food, and we are like, here, you don't know us but eat. I think most of the food was left by the end.

Despite this awkward start, the Breakfast Club continued on. Every Monday morning, volunteers showed up to meet with the students at Overland. Because project coordinator Linda has a full-time job on the opposite side of the city, there were only four volunteers who actually attended the Breakfast Club. All of these volunteers have other jobs but had committed to this ministry. There was only one white volunteer, and Larry was the only volunteer who grew up in this neighborhood. These volunteers were responsible for overseeing all programs, including but not limited to the Monday meetings, that the pastoral staff and Linda created for this outreach ministry.

Pastor Phil was eager to make the most of this ministry opportunity. As he assured the principal, he planned to produce grand events in place of his physical presence at the high school. The pastoral staff and Linda brainstormed different ideas about extending the presence of the church beyond the Breakfast Club. However, due to the pastoral staff living some distance outside of the city and other scheduling conflicts, many of these meetings with Linda occurred over the phone or at the home of the pastor. The volunteers are not involved in these meetings but are expected to carry out the programming designs of the staff. This very segmented chain of command provides little space for volunteers to discuss ideas and expectations for the ministry.

Nonetheless, the lack of the physical presence by those who oversee the ministry—Pastor Phil due to his residence and Linda due to her full-time job—means that the volunteers actually find some freedom on the ground to shape the volunteer experience and the program's efforts to meet the needs of the students. Volunteers find the space to enact their own imaginary of how the church should be in the city and to create opportunities to serve the city how they deem fit.

> They [pastors] were trying to have us go to the kids' homecoming. They were talking about having us do a pre-homecoming thing or something like that. I think they even wanted us to do hair and makeup for the girls. But they never even around, girl! And this ain't no suburban homecoming where people have these ball gowns and limos (laughter). And do they even know how to do these girls' hair? We didn't really plan any of that because we knew it was going to be on us to plan it. Instead we just went to the homecoming and Krista [white volunteer] came with her camera to take some nice pictures for the kids and their families. We just went there to support and Travis and Larry stayed to chaperone. That's what they really needed. They just needed us to be there.
> —Keisha, black volunteer

Making these adjustments on the ground provides volunteers the capacity to resist the authority of the leadership in order to find a functioning way to support the students—students they actually interact with weekly. At times, not surprisingly, these on-the-ground adjustments aren't enough to counter the programming missteps that occur. The divide between the different social locations of the volunteers and the church leaders causes these groups to move through outreach with different privileges and constraints. The divide coupled with the needs of the students at times creates programming pitfalls. Keisha explains:

> One event, they had students fill out information cards and to also put their needs on them. Pregnant girls were told to put medical care and

clothing items, some were encouraged to put legal trouble and legal counsel, others were encouraged to talk about employment. And despite tons of posters with Egg McMuffins on them, encouraging students to come to the Breakfast Club, there was no food provided. When all the cards were collected, there was no follow-up. No calls were made, e-mails sent, nothing. When volunteers asked the pastors, they were told "it's not in our budget."

The lack of follow-through with this event had a trickle-down effect:

So you know at Overland High School they have this Breakfast Club but I found out second or third week they had it that they weren't bringing breakfast. I kind of went off to the leadership. They do now! I said, "what are you doing?" They said, we just want to show up. Who the hell do you think you are? These kids don't know you from anybody. You are not Shaquille O'Neal. Why do you want 1,200 kids to show up because you are here?

Keisha expressed her frustration with the lack of follow-through by the pastoral staff and the overall arrogance that she felt was endemic to the pastoral staff's posturing toward this high school adoption. The four volunteers spent countless hours at the high school as well as on travel time, managing programming events that they had little say in planning, and that were handed down to them with little support and no follow-through. Volunteers were unable to voice their concerns to an absentee pastoral staff, shutting off one way in which they might try to shape the program toward the needs they saw. And yet, the volunteers did not leave the school even when they were denied access to planning meetings; rather, they became more subversive, attaining some of their goals in other ways, such as their efforts at the homecoming. But these disjunctions between staff and volunteers, and between planning and implementation, were abetted by sparse communication between the leadership and volunteers; a result was that the gap between frameworks that outlined the expectation of what could be accomplished and reality widened.

According to several volunteers, the pastors are not held accountable for their lack of investment and dedication to this ministry effort. Although Pastor Phil has pledged devotion and support to the high school's principal, it is the volunteer staff that is left to bear the brunt of any programming mishaps and the non-supportive programming structure. Linda, leader of the ministry, fears the programming oversights come from a misdirected orientation to urban ministry. As Linda speculated earlier, the pastoral staff come from a "suburban mega-church model of big productions." She concluded that part of the gap between planning and execution was the lack of knowledge the pastoral staff brought to urban ministries. The cultural orientation church leaders had toward ministry seemed to be ill-fitted for the current endeavors. This is not to say that people in urban communities don't need events or productions. However, Linda noted that extravagance does not take the place of well thought-out programming that displays an understanding of the target population. The symbolic capital they brought from their suburban mega-church training could not be cashed in at Overland High School. The comments made from the pulpit and in their programming endeavors indicated that they had a limited framework to understand the larger structural barriers that prevent these students from having a successful school year. The racialized urban imaginary of church leaders influences them to engage in the consumption of diversity as a value to grow their congregation without reaching much further. Linda was concerned that their drive for programs, coupled with a lack of knowledge pertaining to urban youth, impeded them from making the Breakfast Club a success.

Spiritual Habitus and Racial Realities

Downtown Church operated as though the Overland High School effort checked off the box as the inner-city programming component for their urban church organization. It is not difficult then to see the influence of their racialized urban imaginary in the ways the pastoral staff approached the program—they literally had to *imagine* who is the urban other, and what meeting their needs might require. The missteps on behalf of the pastoral staff may not be a laissez-faire attitude, or mere arrogant posturing toward volunteers. Rather, it emerged from an overall orientation to urban schools, the urban poor, and outreach ministry that fell outside the lines of what the people in those settings believe they actually need. The church leadership's view of the inner city derived from the comforts of a privileged upbringing and the culture of a suburban neighborhood, with little to no contact with neighborhoods like the West Side of Chicago or schools such as Overland. This may also have been supported by the type of individualist understanding of racial inequality that Emerson and Smith (2000) found common among white evangelical Protestants—a form of a "culture of poverty" perspective. A shielded ignorance about the day-to-day life of the Overland students meant that only particular narratives of students' character, their presumed moral deficiencies, and their overall situation became operable. Good intentions, some energetic volunteers, and even some potentially useful ideas got caught in a web of understandings not well suited to the on-the-ground lives of the target neighborhoods. Linda, the white woman put in place to lead the Overland High School ministry, recalled the disconnect with sadness and some frustration:

> One of the pastors told me, "thank you for going to Overland. You are the light in a dark place and you are showing these kids the love they need" [she starts to get teary eyed]. I'm sorry but it just upsets me. Having love doesn't mean a single-family home in the suburbs. Pastor Emily [pastor's wife] sent that to me on twitter, a twitter message!

The pastors were operating out of broad assumptions about the needs of students without having spent time with them or at the school or with their teachers, and through knowing the school principal mostly on the basketball court. However, it is evident that Linda problematizes the pastor's sentiments, and shows an understanding of the divide between a suburban and urban mind-set as it relates to these children. The pastors are in many ways naive to the dynamics within inner-city neighborhoods, such as structural issues of inequality and racial privilege. The pastor's statements to the congregation reveal an almost clichéd view of the sources and solutions to social problems.

This naiveté is not only evident among the pastoral staff. Keisha recounted a conversation she overheard among some members following a Sunday service. They were talking about Overland High School:

> I have heard someone make the comment, "we have our own prison ministry, it's called Overland High School." And I was like, wooooow, wow! That right there would make me walk out the door. That is crap.

Members of Downtown Church never encounter students from Overland High School unless they volunteer. "Inner-city" residents, meaning people from the poorest, most dangerous neighborhoods, are non-existent at Downtown Church services and events. The distance between these worlds allows stereotypes and racialized assumptions to fill the space between them. Carla, a DC attendee who is black, worried the ministry was becoming more of an event, or a badge of honor. "It's frustrating, you know, it is so showcasey. These are kids with different circumstances, that's it. They ain't worried about you." At some point the naiveté is also met with an ideology and reality of "choice"—that is, the American cultural ideology that individuals' choices are largely responsible for their life circumstances, and then the lived choices that almost all white DC members make not to invest time or energy in the outreach ministry. It is that combination of naiveté and choice that fuels the distance between Overland High School students and Downtown Church officials. Francesca shares,

> It's like the pastors can say they get their hands dirty. 'Cause then we can bring up Overland High School and that is when the suburban thing kicks in [laughter] 'cause they [pastors] are kind of clueless. They are kind of like, we want to come to you but we don't want you coming to us.

I sat down with Linda, the project coordinator, to discuss specifically how she views the ministry and her role. Linda is not part of the pastoral staff but is among the "well-educated" city demographic. She recounted how she is stretched too thin between work and other responsibilities at the church. She regrets that she is not around more to see the Overland ministry through and to provide more input both from and to the pastors.

> To be honest, I was surprised he [Pastor Phil] put me in charge. With all of the other initiatives at the church that he wants me to be a part of, I have no time for Overland High School. It is not that I wouldn't love to invest my time but I work at Kellogg and I can't make that call time at 7 a.m. That is just too much. I know some members of the team are frustrated that I am leading since I am not there, but Phil trusts my experience in education and my degrees. He always says to me that education

matters to people in the city. I know that is part of the reason why he continues to put me in front, so when he is asked about Overland he can say, "the leader of our team has a Master's degree in education."

Indeed, Pastor Phil often mentions that education matters to people in the city. He and his wife did not pursue education after they graduated from high school, and may have some regrets about that. He believes the city is filled with highly educated people—and even equates the urban demographic that DC targets with the idea of well-educated—thus he wants to have well-educated and credentialed people around him, legitimating his philanthropic endeavors. This is different from managing diversity, particularly with the Overland outreach effort. He is not trying to recruit members. Instead he is using the type of cultural capital that comes with middle-class educational credentials to gain entry into powerful circles in the city. Thus, he appointed Linda to lead the ministry. It is not a bad choice, per se, as Linda is talented and dedicated. However, two of the program volunteers who show up every week are actually from that area of the city, and have connections and personal ties to the high school ministry. Larry, in particular, stated that he was part of getting the Overland deal to happen since he is from the area and a former track star at the high school. Like the pastor, Larry does not have any advanced degrees. But Larry does have a long history of volunteer work in the city. Choosing education over experience proved to be a divisive move within the ministry:

> We have been there every Monday and now we have to report to her because she has more degrees than I do? These kids are going to look at her crazy. My team and I decided that we are just going to have to be the bridge to the community because Downtown Church doesn't know what's up!
> —Krista, black volunteer

When constructing the poor in a specific way and constructing what it means to be qualified to serve them, the pastors must balance images, and this can be a slippery slope. They want to be there, they want the church to be involved, they want to be legitimate. And yet, they view their involvement as fundamentally importing things into the city that the city itself lacks, whether that be a certain type of evangelical religion, or material generosity, or cultural resources such as role models. Thus, they simultaneously want to use people from the neighborhoods being served, yet believe those volunteers need supervision and direction from the leadership staff. The discontent and resentment that can result appeared in a number of comments and interviews. Nonetheless, volunteers find a way to resist these understandings within the organization, in part due to the off-site nature of the program direction, and they create their own ways to serve the students at Overland. As Keisha claimed, she and the team continue not only to serve the students but also to act as a bridge to educate church officials about how she believes these students should be served. Keisha and other volunteers enact their own racialized urban imaginary to shape organizational practices and outcomes on the ground level. These volunteer leaders bring forth an alternate set of cultural values and religious identity that are deeply embedded in the structures of race as well. They use this orientation to race, ministry, and the urban landscape to inform church leaders of how they believe a church in the city of Chicago should operate.

City Business

Overland High School outreach ministry is more than a marker of urban church ministries. The school offers church leaders the chance to get involved in the city and allows them entry into circles with key decision makers in Chicago. Downtown Church has bigger dreams for expansion and needs the city's help to achieve its goals. Pastor Phil and Pastor Paul have both expressed how "beneficial" and "profitable" Overland High School has been for them. Paul stated, "We have made some really great contacts in the city when we partnered with the high school. It was a great idea to do it." The nuances of the racialized urban imaginary reveal a market-driven posturing among DC leaders toward their endeavors within the city of Chicago, and their involvement with Overland High School is no different. This assessment of the program's success is in contrast to a previously failed attempt to make moves in the city on the part of the DC leadership.

Prior to adopting Overland, the pastoral staff attempted to go to the City of Chicago to place a bid on some property next to the theater where they now hold worship services. Larry described his reaction after the pastors revealed during a leadership meeting that they did not obtain the necessary support to allow them to purchase the building:

> So they [pastoral staff] came to get a letter to try to get a building, so they are trying to do the political thing, right? They have to appease the alderman so I thought that was funny. I said, "see I told you, you not just gonna roll up in here and be like I got 30 grand." They don't care. How much did you cut to the alderman, how much did you cut the sergeant to get the new building that we want? And I was told Sunday at the meeting that I don't think we got it. And I told them it's 'cause we didn't do the politics. Chicago is Chicago.

A short time after this failed attempt, Pastor Phil announced that the church would be adopting Overland High School and establishing the volunteer program. When basketball season rolled around, Phil invited the principal of Overland to play on the DC basketball team.

> You know we found out that Pastor Phil and Pastor Paul went to a bunch of meetings about Overland with the alderman, none of us [high school volunteers] were invited. He [Pastor Phil] has had his eye on some property in the area and so wanted to go and show his face to hopefully get a recommendation from the alderman.
> —Keisha

As of this writing, the pastoral leadership staff had not returned to Overland since the inaugural breakfast at the first Breakfast Club meeting. Despite their absence at the school, they do seem to be able to leverage the church's program there in order to meet with important city officials. It also remains true that the program volunteers not only find it odd that they are not invited to these meetings, given all of the time they spend on site, but that the church leaders do not attend any events at the high school. Larry stated,

> I joke with the team that it is only the colored people and Kelsey showing up to Overland. It is only me, Travis, Keisha, and Kelsey, and Linda when

it is time for a meeting to give face. But in terms of the homecoming thing, it was just the four of us, in terms of the showcase it was the four of us. Keisha and I got in a convo [conversation] about that, about how Phil and Paul haven't been there since it jumped off. And they always say that they are busy. But that is funny, 'cause they make their own schedule! These are people who make their own schedule so they are choosing to not come.

Larry, Keisha, and Travis and Linda have all expressed some disappointment with the way leadership has handled the programming of the Overland High School ministry. But in that disappointment, these volunteers find a way to make this program fit the needs of the target population. Larry, in particular, sees the benefits of volunteering at Overland:

I do more for my people with this white guy out in front of me than I was doing before I came here. And that is the beauty behind this. We are building something here. Phil is a jerk, but he is a blessed jerk.

Larry expressed his relationship to the church and outreach leadership as an exchange of legitimation. He validates their credibility in being in the high school, and their organizational resources and symbolic presence give him opportunities to do things that he was not able to before. Larry further explained that he had always wanted to give back to his neighborhood and to Overland but never had the platform. He says this, even considering all of his community service and his friendship with the high school principal that he outlined earlier. Larry clearly believed that Pastor Phil needed him to gain the trust of the principal of Overland, but he also acknowledged that aligning himself with the church has given him in return the legitimation he needs. The long history between inner cities and church ministries offers Larry the edge he needs to achieve his own goals for *his* community. Larry's interpretation of this exchange in legitimation works as an example of the racial utility of volunteers being turned on its head. The racial utility of the worker now works in the favor of those being used in order to achieve a substantial mark on the lives of the disenfranchised in the city. Larry uses his racial utility as a form of capital—making sure that the church is truly for those in the city and not just for the upwardly mobile. It may not be a fully equal exchange, but neither is it completely one-sided.

The Business of Outreach

Downtown Church set its sights on the local basketball league and a high school outreach as fertile ground that would allow it to expand its name in the city. Church officials are trying to be a part of the city of Chicago, just as much as they are trying to reach out in the city. They do this by attempting to enter into city politics with the basketball team and the outreach ministry. Within their efforts, we find nuances within the racialized urban imaginary that work to establish each group's orientation to church ministry. On one level, there is the identity of the church. Downtown Church seeks to be seen as an established, authentic, urban organization that is to be taken seriously in the city. But in order to become so, they must learn the "rules" of the city—both politically and culturally—in order to effectively establish that identity. There is a steep learning curve that money and resources by themselves cannot buy. Church officials come from the "suburbs," which is often code for white, homogeneous, and clueless about city politics and racial privilege. There is a cultural deficit for church leaders for which their existing cultural capital is non-transferable. The pastoral leadership is unfamiliar with the politics of the city, unfamiliar with the larger structural issues that create schools such as Overland, and seemingly unfamiliar with the race work done on their behalf by their volunteers.

The Urban Exchange

In an effort to gain the symbolic capital and cultural resources they need, church officials, with the help of volunteers, embarked on different outreach efforts to get their name out in the city and to establish themselves. While outreach ministries are a common component to evangelical churches, Overland presented different challenges that church officials were neither familiar with nor prepared to handle. They lacked detailed knowledge of the residential segregation patterns that concentrated poverty in the West Side near Overland. They did not have deep knowledge about policies of education reform and resourcing that prevent the high school from providing adequate services. These, and other factors associated with low-income areas, prevented church officials from planning effectively and kept the program from being an unambiguous success. Individualistic views that explain why students are late, rather than recognizing the economic realities facing students who often have no bus fare to get to school, or have to work nights, or who are faced with taking care of family members or their own children, create a further divide between the church and the students. The cultural deficits among church leaders ultimately placed the volunteer staff in the middle.

These endeavors by the church are multifaceted, reflecting a combination of differences in social location, colorblindness in thinking about individual race relations, and the racialized urban imaginary that provides the overall vision of how a church in the city should respond to its neighbors. Both congregants and church officials are together in wading through these outreach ministries with different privileges and constraints. The results are social exchanges, and the interdependent nature of the varied social and cultural capital means that both groups are needed to make these outreach programs work. This keeps the cyclical nature of exchange going. Congregants and church officials become the gatekeepers for each other's success and shape their ability to maneuver within the confines of the ministry and politics of the city. Certainly these are not fully equal exchanges, as the church leadership and the member volunteers do not start with the same resources either in terms of quantity or their social value. White, middle-class privilege is the limiting context. However, volunteers can resist the directives, and often hidden power, of the church leadership on the ground by making their own way. Nonetheless, they also deal with the brunt of the program's poor resourcing and direction. It is not easy to get to the school at 7 a.m. every week and to facilitate a program with few resources, especially when they themselves have little say in how to make it better. This outreach ministry connects the church to the city, and it also reveals different conceptions of the city, the urban poor, and the place each has at Downtown Church.

Service and Hustle in the City

In their efforts to expand their physical location and their name in the city, Downtown Church encounters different dimensions of consuming the city. Participating in a basketball league and outreach ministry are not just a political ploy but also feed the appetite of those who are searching for an "urban experience." The distance the pastors and many congregants have between themselves and these communities allows them to experience a "pickup game" or an "inner-city" school from the comfort of the privileges offered by the church. As church leaders serve the city they are also consuming the "other" in the process. The basketball team and the inner-city school offer pastoral leaders a way to wed their need for authenticity in a new urban environment to the cultural standards of evangelical Protestant ministry and outreach—established practices and customs in their religious tradition. An inner-city ministry is a common feature of urban churches in large cities. Overland High School offers Downtown Church continued legitimacy as an authentic urban space while helping them further solidify their place in the city.

In these exchanges, on the court and in the school, we see a swapping of symbolic and "color" capital. Racial utility is used to the advantage of volunteer leaders on both ends to advance the endeavors of both volunteers and church leaders, if unequally. The privilege associated with the church leadership's whiteness allows African American volunteers such as Larry to go into his community, while the racial utility of his and other volunteers' blackness helps church officials to find favor in the eyes of city leaders. These uneven exchanges show us how the city and churches are often colored and classed in different spaces, offering privilege to different social locations at any given time. Being affiliated with this wealthy white pastor and his church offers Larry access into a space he has tried to get into for years. And vice-versa, his capacity to come back to the community with a certain authority and legitimacy provides color capital for the church, and helps them to get in with the principal and alderman.

Being a church in the city often requires a "hustle." Particularly for Downtown Church, and its parent suburban mega-church, there is a hustle to be the best, to have the most land, to reproduce their suburban success by becoming something big in the city. Thus there are always negotiations that must take place, a constant tug and pull between the desire to be in the city and make a name for themselves as a church, but also as a group of outsiders wanting to belong in "the big city." And yet, the position of church leaders, as those in charge, as those with the knowledge and faith to make it as a church but also transform their setting, cannot be too challenged by giving too much authority to those already in the community. If that were to happen, it would raise the question of why the new church is needed in the first place. Thus, there is a certain reserve, an unwillingness to let go of the reins, even as there is the professed desire to fit in. They must succeed at the "hustle" while not being taken by it.

These dynamics have produced some paradoxical outcomes. The pastoral staff invests in the basketball league and the high school, but can be accused of too much "flash" and not enough "follow-through." The leadership uses local members to get them into these settings, then tries to direct the programming at a distance, in turn giving the on-the-ground volunteers the paradoxical opportunity to use the white privilege of the church leadership in order to get into a school and work in the ways they think are best. The volunteers in part challenge the leadership's racialized urban imaginary, and often resent it, yet at the same time take advantage of it for their own purposes. Power and resistance both work simultaneously alongside intersecting imaginaries to shape the religious practices and cultural values of the organization.

As leaders and congregants continue to build their congregational identity within the racialized city of Chicago, we shift the lens from outward endeavors to inward bonds. Exploring interracial romance and inclusion within the congregation furthers our understanding of how the racialization of the urban landscape contours the religious identities and organizational posturing of Downtown Church.

5

"Swirl Babies"

I don't know why people don't date in the church. I'm always
surprised because there are so many young, attractive people
here. There are black men, white men, Asian men, you name it.
—Clarissa, church member

The racialized urban imaginary of Downtown Church leaders and congregants extends well beyond marketing, organizational practices, and
the congregation's community engagement. It also finds its way into
the private lives of its members. As Downtown Church attracts congregants with a religious life centered on urban nightlife, sensuality, and
the potential to "find a hot wife," tensions arise as the pastoral staff and
congregants construct the norms of courtship and dating within their
congregation. These tensions reveal the thresholds of *managed diversity*
and the boundaries, restrictions, and opportunities these thresholds create for congregants in their romantic lives. The ways in which church
members and leaders understand and respond to interracial coupling
are inextricably tied to larger ideas about gender, community, identity, and place. Shifting our attention from the organizational practices
that promote the church to the interpersonal interactions within it, we
find the social dimensions of managing diversity in the private lives of
congregants. Investigating interracial romantic relationships among
congregants allows us to see how members and pastors adapt the cultural value of religious coupling in a racialized urban location.

It is not unusual, of course, for religious congregations to have an
intense interest in the romantic lives of their congregants, at least in
general terms. Religion in the United States has always been concerned
about regulating sexuality through inculcating moral values and enforc-
ing normative practices. And churches are always interesting in "reproducing the faith," much of which is done through the literal biological
reproduction of children by church members. Marriages and baptism,

religious education and confirmation, are common to most, if not all, religious groups, done with more or less formal, and more or less liturgically sanctioned rituals. Further, a congregation such as Downtown Church, which specifically focuses on attracting young, usually single, people to its services, will need to address the romantic relationships that inevitably ensue. Young adulthood is an identity moment that regularly leads to romantic love and family formation. It is part of the lifeblood of the congregation, and when well managed can be a tremendous attraction to potential congregants. As Downtown Church caters to the young adult, romantic partnering is a key component in the equation.

And yet, Downtown Church must address these common issues with a somewhat distinct focus. The church's careful production of congregational diversity, and its ethos of cultivating the style of downtown entertainment life, shape how it will deal with sexuality, marriage, and family formation. Further, interracial sexual and romantic relationships have long been a hot-button issue within the American racial order. Some states in the United States had laws forbidding interracial marriages as late as 1967. Even today, popular opinion surveys consistently find that interracial marriage taboos are some of the last racial prejudices to fall.

Downtown Church leaders create their congregation as, in part, a safe place to consume racial diversity as an extension of the urban experience. And interracial sexuality has long been considered dangerous by many Americans. Thus, the church puts itself at the intersection of these opposing impulses and deliberately courts a certain tension around dating, sex, and marriage. For the pastoral leadership, the managed diversity approach to maximizing the racial utility of their members makes interracial romantic relationships another site to manage in their experiment with urban ambiance.

Four vignettes focused directly on interracial partnering within the congregation will help reveal how the racialized urban imaginary of the congregational leaders shapes the social context in which the congregants meet each other and perhaps become romantically involved. These dynamics, in turn, provide the contours within which the congregants navigate romantic relationships in their pursuit of inclusion, relationship-building, and congregational diversity in the urban religious market. Analysis of these experiences with interracial dating and sexual encounters among congregants reveals the implicit and sometimes contradictory forms of boundary maintenance within the consumption of diversity for this urban congregation. These four stories offer a range of insights extending the notion of managed diversity beyond organizational practices to the maintenance of boundaries between congregants and within their public and private lives. These interactions offer a rich source of information on interracial partnerships, which are inextricably tied to the *quality* and *type* of diversity that is acceptable in church located in a racialized urban context.

Black Men with Potty Mouths: Class, Status, and Race

Linda and I were in the middle of an interview. Linda, as you recall, is a white woman who works as an educator in the city; she has a MA degree and prides herself on her "very cosmopolitan lifestyle." She began to explain her relationships with the pastors on staff, recounting that they elevated her quickly into leadership positions, and took her to conferences as well as international trips to see other churches abroad. She quickly became a favorite of the leadership; as she reflected, "The pastors were always so supportive of me and really allowed me to use my voice and my training in developing the children's ministry."

Linda then began to focus her attention on the moment when she was confronted by the pastors about her boyfriend, a black man who works as a security guard.

> As much as the pastors love me, they definitely don't love my boyfriend. It's actually unsettling for them. It's like here is this really successful white woman and she has a boyfriend who is a cop and security. They met him briefly. Pastor Phil literally said hello to him and that was it. Pastor Paul didn't even say anything. After my guy left, he [Pastor Phil] immediately went on saying things like "you shouldn't be with a guy like that" or "you can do better than him" or "you have worked so hard, why would you want to go backwards?" I was shocked. Look, I'm no flowery virgin, okay? I have had relationships since I was young, at 25, 27, 30. But the pastors don't get that. They are so sheltered. They think that if you're not marrying a pastor then no guy is worthy. Just because my guy works security and doesn't look like he has a lot of money, and has potty mouth, that he isn't good enough [she begins to cry]. I just can't believe they would say

such things about him. They don't even know him and they won't even take the time to get to know him. They literally said one word to him, that's it, one word! I try to invite him or bring him around and they [the pastors] always tell me to come alone. I won't put him in that position for people to judge him before they know him. All they know is that he is black and doesn't look like he comes from much, and that is enough for them. They literally have never spoken to him or taken the time to get to know him.

Linda's description of her encounter with the pastors offers a glimpse into the social and cultural boundaries that are steeped in racialized and classed notions of courtship and paternalism. In the courtship style of forming romantic relationships, Pastor Phil inserts himself as the "father." This father is vested with the power to help the couple, or in this case the woman, determine when and how the relationship should progress through various intimacy levels (Irby 2013). Implied in this positioning is the expectation that the couple is to seek out this leadership and guidance. However, according to Linda, Pastor Phil inserted himself into this position with no consent on her part. Courtney Irby (2013) argues that debates about courtship and dating permeate the emotional and conceptual background of evangelical Protestantism, as young (white) evangelicals construct and pursue relationships. It seems clear that Linda and Pastor Phil have different conceptions of courtship and dating. Linda perceives the pastors as having a very narrow understanding of dating life—the goal is to date minimally and ideally marry a pastor. She doesn't necessarily approach her dating life from this particular evangelical lens, and yet she still seeks the approval of her spiritual leaders to the point where she is deeply hurt when they do not approve of her partner.

The pastoral staff's implied views of romantic partnership express to Linda a traditional gender lens about paternal authority, combined with a racialized ideology that some call color-blind racism (Bonilla-Silva 2006). As Linda described it, one short interaction was enough to convince the leadership that her boyfriend was not fit for her. And they communicated to her fairly explicitly. She recounted the pastors' concerns as mostly being expressed about the couple's uneven socioeconomic standing, with a clear hierarchy that means that doing "better" in the relationship was associated with doing better economically. But she also believed there was more than just an income difference. Part of the pastors' discomfort stemmed from their assumptions about his social class and the culture they perceive embedded within a racialized class structure.

Social science research has shown that social class and status are concerns for interracial couples due in part to the racialized sentiments those class standings hold for each couple (Holland 2012; McClintock 2010). Claiming that the central concern is the cultural differences that accompany a lower socioeconomic status (as Linda alludes, her partner is a security guard and has a "potty mouth") is one way to negate the racialized prejudices people have toward interracial couples. While difficult to conclude definitively, Pastor Phil's concerns, as expressed to Linda, fit that pattern. Concern for socioeconomic differences also dismisses the structural barriers many African American men face in the workforce, barriers that disproportionately concentrate them in lower wage work (Royster 2003). The pastors attempt a color-blind approach to deterring Linda from dating her black boyfriend by framing their concerns in terms of class, and within terms of concern and endearment.

The pastoral staff appears to have fairly specific guidelines for whom they deem as an appropriate partner for Linda. Yet Linda challenges their sentiments in part by calling upon her own history and preferred lifestyle. For example, she described herself as "not a flowery virgin" and therefore not interested in marrying a (white) pastor. Linda implicitly evaluated the moralized gendered and racial assumptions used by the pastors. By noting that the pastors are sheltered, and don't know anything about her boyfriend or even really anything about her, Linda offered a gendered critique of paternalism in the church while also noting the implicit racial undertones of the interaction. The pastors appear to be paternalistically "protecting" a white woman who by her own admission is not interested in being protected from this black man, but would rather be respected for her own decisions.

After completing the interview, Linda thanked me for "our therapy session." Her emotions were still running high; as Linda dabbed her eyes with a tissue she said, "I can't believe I cried when I was talking about my guy. I didn't think they [the pastors] got to me like that." This is some striking evidence that the pastors have significant influence and are prominent in shaping the culture of the congregation, as well as the experiences, emotions, and journeys of the congregants. Not having the support of her pastor really affects the way Linda experiences her relationship. She went on to explain that she has trouble talking about her relationship with people at the church because she doesn't want anyone to get the wrong idea about the pastor and his leadership. Linda confessed that she also doesn't feel comfortable talking about this incident to her friends because they will question why she gives so much of her time to the church. Ultimately, the discouragement from the pastoral staff has kept Linda silent and her partner absent from church functions. At a very intimate level, the power and authority of the pastor allow a racialized judgment of relationships to penetrate into the private and emotional lives of the congregants. Having buy-in to the congregation makes it difficult for congregants to critique the pastor publicly. For Linda, the tension creates instances of emotional trauma and isolation (Moon 2013). As Downtown Church's pastors manage diversity through gendered expectations of dating, congregants must manage their emotions in the face of issues of power and race. As we see in the next vignette, it is not only white women who are subjected to this framework of relationship control. Nor do color-blind exchanges only permeate through white-on-white interaction. Gender, class, and race intersect in different ways in the racialized context of romantic partnership and interpersonal interactions within the church.

"You Can't Talk to Him": Controlling the Relationship Market

Evan is one of the church interns. He is a young, white Midwestern guy in his early twenties. I often asked Evan for insights into the pastoral inner circle, the day-to-day operation of the church, along with general views about young people, religion, and adulthood. As a key informant he was invaluable in recommending members for interviews. It was not uncommon for me to talk with Evan before or after Sunday worship services.

One Sunday after service had ended, Pastor Phil spots Evan and I talking. He walks directly up to us, faces me and says, "You can't talk to him." His delivery is abrupt and dry. It is unclear if he is joking or if he is publicly rep-

rimanding me. Quickly the pastor gently grabs my arm, walks me over to another part of the lobby, to Bryant, a young black man who is part of the worship ministry. Pastor Phil addresses me again. "This is who you should be talking to. Go ahead Bryant, ask for her number." Pastor Phil smiles and stands next to me. Both Bryant and I are looking at each other, confused. I briefly scan the lobby to ease some of the tension. The lobby is full of mostly singles. I recognize that Bryant is not a convenient choice but a deliberate one (do I need to say more here?). Neither one of us know what to do in this moment, handcrafted by the pastor. Bryant politely takes out his phone and pretends to fumble around, delaying the moment he must ask for my information. Pastor Phil smiles contently, turns and walks away. I reassure Bryant it is unnecessary that we trade information. I hand him a flyer for participation in this study, he smiles in relief, and we go our separate ways.
—Field note

The following week, I followed up with Bryant and Evan independently. Bryant claimed the pastor had been "on the hunt to find me a wife" and that is most likely the reason for the exchange. As we have seen, the pastors are not shy about their desire for the church to be a place where men can "find a hot wife." However, it is apparent that that search must be conducted within the parameters of same-race partnership and with the pastor at the helm of the pursuit. Further, all relationships between men and women are perceived as "proto-romantic," irrespective of the situation or a preexisting friendship. Bryant admitted that he is actually dating someone outside of the church but wants to keep it under wraps until it gets a bit more serious.

Bryant excused the actions of the pastor as a result of buy-in to the evangelical assumption that marriage is a necessity in adult life (Irby 2014). The impetus to protect women (and marry them off) that is often a criticism of conservative (religious) groups is also applied to men here. The entire pastoral staff of Downtown Church is married and Pastor Phil himself was married when he was just 22 years old. As Jorstad (1993:96) notes, "Marriage as evangelicals understand it is for most persons simply programmed into the biological, spiritual, and mental makeup of humankind. God intends that it be a blessing, a way of carrying out the divine mandates of the Bible, and a means of self-understanding." One of the main reasons for starting the Downtown Church as a congregation plant was to attract young, single, unchurched adults and give them an unconventional space to worship. While the pastors attempt to capture elements of city life in their organization, they bring with them traditional frames about partnership, implicitly and sometimes explicitly promoting them within the congregation. These conservative worldviews do not completely align with those of the congregants, as the majority of members are young singles in their twenties and early thirties, and many are not from the evangelical faith tradition where this is so normative. The pastoral staff has a conceptually different framework regarding the purpose and function of single life than many congregants. Thus, the pastoral staff creates a solution they can understand for the "problem" of young, unattached women and men—find them spouses. The racialized urban imaginary, however, is structured such that the pastors go a step further and consider race as a main signifier in what counts as appropriate.

It becomes clear, however, that there is little room for interracial relationship building or interaction in the church's framework. The pastoral staff is consuming the cosmopolitan urban way of life but only within certain limits. As is made clear by the episode with Evan and Bryant, Pastor Phil's actions communicate a particular stand on race and gender in romantic relationships. At Downtown Church, conservative notions of marriage as legitimating adulthood support dating and sexuality but in a very specific, racialized way. Getting married is recognized as symbolizing something larger, so it has to be done in the appropriate manner. While the conservative religious script on marriage is not necessarily held up among congregants, it is the explanation Bryant accepts for the pastor's actions. While previous literature takes seriously how pastoral authority shapes and constrains the process of romantic partnership for church congregants, it is important to push further to consider how these practices are intentionally racialized in a context where people could choose partners of another race.

When I discussed the event with Evan, he attributed the experience to Pastor Phil's "socially awkward" personality: "I'm not sure why he would do something like that. He can be strange sometimes, like he is trying too hard. I don't know, he wasn't making sense that day." Evan's explanation of the encounter was ambivalent toward the pastor's actions. In one way, Evan's response can be viewed as an example of color-blind ideology in practice as he disregards any racial undertones to the interaction. Yet, on the other hand, Evan's ambivalence may also serve as a form of resistance. Ambivalence can be a powerful tool actors use in order to not be complicit in controversial ideologies (Avishai 2008). Read that way, Evan's ambivalence toward the pastor's approach may be a subtle way of affirming interracial interaction in a space where the organizational authority does not. We call attention to this ambivalence, and its "both/ and" qualities, as an insight into the overall practice and structure of the church, and the often paradoxical ways the leadership and congregants' conflicting racialized urban imaginaries toward interracial dating affect how each operates in the social space.

It is important to note that there was never a conversation about dating between Evan and me; it seems that the mere threat of a relationship developing out of a casual conversation prompted the pastor to act. Regulating romantic relationships (or in this case, the assumed potential for a relationship) through physical means or pressure from authority implicitly constructs interracial relationships as wrong, or at the very least, to be avoided. Rejecting interracial romance in a diverse, urban environment reiterates the consumptive orientation to diversity rather than an intimate one. While the urban environment is viewed, in part, as sensual and alluring by church officials, it is only done so within the confines of same-racial romantic interactions.

In sum, Downtown Church's pastors attempt to manage diversity within the church even at the interpersonal level, through patrolling interracial interactions among women and men alike. The racialized and heteronormative paternalism is enacted differently across gender but aims for the same outcome—same-race, heterosexual romantic partnerships. I perceived continued surveillance by the pastor after that one encounter. Whether that was also true for Bryant and Evan is not known directly, and I never pushed Pastor Phil to declare his opinions about interracial relationships directly. But Bryant's reluctance to let his existing relationship with a non-church member be known suggests some concern about church scrutiny.

The pastors are not always successful in their attempts to control the relationship practices of congregants. There are those in the church who not only are involved in interracial relationships but also pushed beyond dating to marriage and children. These cases could raise some question as to whether race boundaries are as defended as we allege. However, when such boundaries are breached, the workings of managed diversity can be more clearly revealed. As the following vignette demonstrates, multiracial families fall outside the constructs of diversity that the pastoral staff find comfortable, and their attempts to cope with those situations show the parameters of their vision and the limits of their influence. It complicates the overall religious identity of the church.

Swirl Baby

Grant is African American and a former greeter in the church. He and his brother are prominent club promoters in Chicago. Lydia is a white woman from a well-to-do family in the suburbs of Chicago. She is a former greeter as well. Grant and Lydia used to be fixtures at the front door of the theater for worship services, greeting everyone as they entered. But their presences dropped off somewhat suddenly. And then, one Sunday they arrived together, and Lydia was noticeably pregnant. The lobby was filled with whispers as they walked by. Are they married? How far along is she? When did they start dating?

Fairly quickly, Pastor Phil walked up to the couple. He looked directly at Lydia's stomach and then addressed the couple.

PASTOR PHIL: I had no idea. How long had this been going on for? How did this all happen? I wish you had told me you were getting married. Why wouldn't you tell me something like that? It all seemed to happen so fast.
GRANT: It did happen fast. We were only married four months ago.
PASTOR PHIL: I would have liked to be involved. I could have been involved in the wedding at least. I could have conducted the ceremony.
GRANT: My bad, but Lydia's family friend did our ceremony.

Pastor Phil's rapid-fire questions are met with awkward smiles and laughs from Grant and Lydia. As with the interaction described above, Phil's dry delivery made it difficult to tell if he was sarcastically addressing the couple or was truly troubled. As we have seen in the earlier vignettes, Pastor Phil assumed an authoritative role in the romantic partnership—quizzing them more like an authority than a friend. He seemed to be dismayed that the couple would leave him out of such an important part of their lives. The couple tried to reassure the pastor with a brief apologetic phrase, and then explained the family connection to the person who conducted the ceremony. To which Pastor Phil replied, "I could have at least gotten an invite." The couple continued to smile and giggle a bit, and threw up their hands as if to wave the white flag. But Pastor Phil never congratulated them on getting married or Lydia's pregnancy. His desire to be recognized—especially recognized as an authority—seemed to swamp his capacity to follow basic social niceties. Finally, Grant politely reminded the pastor that they have other friends in the congregation that they would like to visit with before they leave. The pastor nods, but added, "I still would have liked to know what was going on between you two beforehand." After Pastor Phil departed, other church members surrounded the couple, squealing, laughing, and congratulating them.

As friends gathered round and talked, they also asked questions regarding the timeline of Grant and Lydia's union. How long were they dating before they got married? Did they get married before Lydia became pregnant? How far along is she? Grant and Lydia were evasive with many of the details, not wanting to divulge when they started dating, but were forthcoming in saying they were married shortly after they found out Lydia was pregnant. After they had spent time visiting, they left.

Grant and Lydia did not return until a few months after their baby was born. And their return revealed once again the tensions within the lived racial and gender order of Downtown Church as it relates to organizational values and orientations to race within an urban setting. An extensive passage from my field notes describes it:

Grant and Lydia are here with baby in tow. They quietly and discretely slide into the row behind me. Everyone is seated in the sanctuary. Pastor Phil reads the announcements and then introduces the guest speaker. Kenny is a tall, black man from the Midwest. Immediately, Kenny expresses how much he loves preaching at Downtown Church. He boasts of its uniqueness, its style, and how special a place it is to have a room full of racially diverse, young adults in the city of Chicago.

Then he says, "And your pastor made me aware that the church had its first 'swirl baby.'" He then swiftly points to where Lydia and Grant are sitting. The spotlight shines on their stunned faces. The guest speaker then charges the couple, "Hold up your *swirl* so we can all see *it*." At this point Pastor Phil is standing on his feet, clapping, encouraging the crowd to clap. Most in the congregation are laughing, clapping and cheering, while some shake their heads, placing their hands over their face, or just sit in silence.

The couple obliges. Grant stands and lifts his infant daughter, similar to when Mufasa raises Simba to the pride in *The Lion King*. The cheering subsides and the couple sits down. The spotlight returns to Kenny. After the services, I overhear Grant talking to Lydia and another white member. He keeps repeating the question, "Is my kid a swirl baby? Am I supposed to call my kid a swirl? The pastor told Kenny to call my kid a swirl in front of the church. So I guess that is what people are calling my kid?"

Neither Grant nor Lydia seem amused with the entire ordeal. Rather, the public proclamation of their child as a "swirl baby" left them questioning the identity of their child and mulling over the pastor's role in promoting that characterization of their family.

—Field note

The evening's episode is revealing on a number of levels. First was the public exhibition of a multiracial family and their new child. Grant and Lydia were not open with their relationship in the church before getting married, and had been gone for three months after Pastor Phil confronted them when they first returned. Yet they were singled out and put on display during a worship service. It is true that there are few couples with children in DC, so a new baby could be seen as a special event, but those other children are not put on display. The pastoral leadership may have intended this to be a moment of celebration of and for the couple, but given the context and their previous experience, it was clear they did not perceive it that way.

The language used in the episode is also critical to understand, in that language can function to isolate or celebrate, normalize or alienate, just as a public display does. Announcing the infant as a "swirl baby" gives direction into how the church leadership constructs interracial couples and their children; they appear as a novelty—outside of the norm. *Swirl baby* communicates something very different about interracial coupling, intimacy, and family than what is mentioned for same-race families. Multiracial children are defined in different ways than their single-race

counterparts, revealing the normative boundaries around intimate partnering and sex. To dismiss the term as "slang" ignores, and even con-
ceals, the authority and privilege of those outside of multiracial families
to characterize the family and its identity.

The public display of Grant and Lydia, as a couple and then as a family, reveals the threshold of managed diversity. A swirl baby could function to represent the ultimate in internalizing the diversity that marks a
city. However, such a child also undermines the visual diversity that the
church promotes, and it clearly marks a failure to keep that diversity in
clearly delineated categories. Moreover, a biracial child represents per-
manence. The sexual union of an interracial couple represents a type
of approval for interracial interaction that compromises the religious
identity that the church leadership has worked diligently to cultivate.

These experiences left a mark. Grant and Lydia left the church. I kept
in touch with them throughout the duration of the study, and was even
invited to Lydia's graduation party from law school. At the party, I inquired as to why they left the church. Both expressed a "lack of community" as the reason for leaving. They explained that now that they had a
family, they want a church that is more family friendly, with couples and
families that look "more like them." They also assured me that they will
never refer to their daughter as a "swirl baby." Interracial coupling falls
out of the bounds of the racialized urban imaginary of church leaders
at DC, resulting in the loss of membership among those who pursue a
truly integrated, multiracial lifestyle.

A Community of Outlaws

From field notes:

> One evening after service, James pulls me aside to see if I want to join a
> group of members for a night out on the town. He pulls me in close and
> says, "you can come if you promise you won't tell anyone at the church
> what you see." I agree and so he gives me the location to a lounge down-
> town. When I walk into the lounge, there is a section roped off toward
> the back and seated inside are members of Downtown Church and some
> of their friends. The bottles of alcohol James ordered are just arriving.
> James begins pouring drinks for everyone as I walked up. A few faces are

visibly shocked to see me, but I am immediately greeted with hugs and handshakes.

I can't put my finger on it at first. Many of the members of the church, including the pastors, go out for a drink, frequent lounges and dance clubs, so I know it isn't the alcohol or the location that has me sworn to secrecy. As everyone begins to settle into our secluded area, it becomes very clear that these members are not here with their friends but with their romantic partners. Couples begin to pair up, hold hands, sit on laps, and dance together. Every couple is interracial, some of which are members of the volunteer leadership team. I shadowed many of these individuals for months and have interviewed the majority of the people in the room but never once were their partners ever mentioned. It then becomes clear—James invited me to a secret meeting of interracial couples at the church. James quickly notices my wheels turning and gestures me over to the edge of the rope.

JAMES: Now you see why I told you not to say anything? None of us want anyone to know at the church. You know the pastors trip about stuff like that.

BARRON: Do they? What do they say to you?

JAMES: They want to be all in your business telling you who to date and who not to date. We don't want to hear that. It's unfortunate, but we would rather do things like this and meet on our own than hear a lecture from Pastor.

BARRON: Is Pastor Phil opposed to people in leadership dating?

JAMES: (with an eyebrow raised and a smirk) No, it's because he doesn't want to see all these black men with their white women.

BARRON: Has he said something to you specifically before?

JAMES: He doesn't have to say it explicitly. In so many words, you know? Like telling us who we should date but it's always a black girl or someone of your same race even if he knows that you and a white girl would be perfect for each other. He has made explicit comments to some of the others. It's crazy because it's like, wouldn't you want people from your congregation dating? He always says we about relationships and doing life together here, so what is more like that than dating? That's really doing life together (laughter). But there is a white guy with an Asian female and they [pastors] always talk about what a great guy he is and how great they are together. It's just annoying. You know it doesn't feel comfortable. So some of us just decided if we are going to be a mixed couple we wouldn't do it at the church. My boy manages this spot and a few others. He is real good about hooking us up. And these spots we know the pastor won't be at after service. It's a cool little community we have.

BARRON: Why do you think the pastors' support some interracial couples over others?

JAMES: I don't know but whatever the reason is, it's whack. Maybe he is jealous or insecure, I'm not sure. But it is disappointing because we have some really good men at the church.

BARRON: How long have you been meeting like this?

JAMES: It's been a while, probably about eight months or so. Once most of us were in leadership and we would hang out a lot and then you catch feelings. But after being discouraged we just decided to meet on our own. We hang out outside of church sometimes but since we all live in different parts of the city, Sundays are usually the day we are all in the same place so we just go out after. It works for us. Remember don't say anything (laughs).[1]

James's words, and the very fact of the secretive couples' meetings, indicate that many in the church see the church leadership as being overly controlling and trying to manage interracial relationships. And they note that if those relationships might be between black men and white women the staff communicates clear disapproval. James ironically references the church motto of "doing life together" and how these efforts contradict it. Further, even the less-official but clearly communicated message of "find a hot wife" seems to be on hold if it involves interracial interactions. This calls into question the *type* of interracial interactions that are celebrated within the church and the *quality* of those interactions in the shared space. It becomes evident that the power dynamics associated with racial utility shape both social and organizational outcomes for church members. It allows one group to be consumed rather than to participate in the diversity they are helping to facilitate. The pastors have effectively created a context that makes it uncomfortable for members, specifically black men and white women, to express their romantic feelings and receive support. Like Bryant in the example earlier in this chapter, James clearly perceived raced boundaries that set interracial unions with a black partner apart from the rest. But much like Evan, James had some difficulty reconciling the contradictions, and ended up explaining the pastors' attitudes and actions as insecurity or jealousy—perhaps unflattering, but not a serious charge of racism.

Like Evan and Bryant, James was hesitant to critique the pastor outright. James alluded to power and racial dynamics that define his experiences, but was careful to guard his speech. It is often difficult to reconcile tensions that occur if a spiritual leader warrants critique. If congregants do not feel like they have the space to disagree, the impact can be traumatic (Wilkins 2008). Again, not having a space to discuss transgressions within congregations proves detrimental. As previously stated, the *problem of race* (Becker 1998) cannot be solved without a space for discourse. Likewise, the dominant ideologies and discourses on race that exist within the congregation undoubtedly play a role in both the couples' responses and their perceptions of the pastors' views.

There was one black-Latinx couple at the evening gathering, while the other couples were black men and white women, with a total of eight couples in attendance. All were heterosexual. James said that a few other couples were not present because of schedules or because they recently broke up. Throughout the night, others shared similar stories of pastors' disapproval of their relationship, or trying to steer them toward same-race partners. Ironically, many of the couples stated that these occurrences brought them closer to each other, providing a sense of community. They may have resented the intrusion or disapproval of the pastoral staff, and they did not push back directly, by voicing objections or even by leaving the church. Rather, this group of dating "outlaws" built an alternative space for community while continuing their commitment to the congregation they helped to build.

In many ways, these couples are deeply affected by the church's de facto boundaries that push them to keep their relationships out of organizational sight. Their invisibility reinforces the notion that specific types of interracial couples are outside of the norm of romantic relationships and beyond the norms conceptualized in the racialized urban imaginary of the pastoral staff. The social world of Downtown Church does not make room for these couples, and when they become visible it produces the public awkwardness, and ultimate disaffection, that Grant and Lydia experienced. At Downtown Church, raced bodies are prized as an important dimension of being an urban church, but are to be consumed within the safe space of the church. Action that would lead to dating, sexual encounters, or marriage seemingly falls outside of that space for church leaders. Managing diversity through the management of interracial unions is one way to ensure that diversity remains safely contained within the constructs of the pastoral staff's racialized urban imaginary as it pertains to meshing church and the city.

Dating within Secured Borders: Power, Ambivalence, and Community

Aside from offering companionship, romantic relationships help to define social norms that revolve around the intersections of gender, race, sexuality, marriage, and the family. Exploring the social context that defines dating for members of Downtown Church addresses the extent to which members can be involved not only in the church but also in each others' lives. It is made clear in the stories told by church members that there is a very particular construct of dating and family within this urban-based congregation. Whether it is defining a biracial child as a swirl baby, physically moving members to keep them from having contact with each other, or directly addressing the distaste for a black partner (even if the comments were not about race), the pastors have given many members the clear sense that interracial coupling is outside their conception of the church community. The authority of the white leadership staff coupled with their racialized urban lens effectively defines the boundaries of race and the meaning of race in their congregation.

Counter responses from congregants, however, provide conflicting narratives of the *quality* and *type* of racial integration and diversity that is imagined appropriate in this urban-based religious organization. It is within this tension that we explore the interpersonal and social context church leaders have created and the boundaries and opportunities these contexts create. The vignettes draw attention to the gendered dimension of interracial dating, and the racialized dimensions of the tactics that reproduce organizational boundaries around racial interactions. Pastors enact their racialized urban imaginary regarding the role of race in the city, which results in managing diversity through asserting pastoral power in the dating matters of their congregants. The consequences of these dynamics leave some church members feeling outside any collective sense of religious belonging. Within this exploration emerges a thematic discussion of power, ambivalence, and community.

Power: Rewriting Racial Realities and the Naturalization of Same-Race Couples

The traditionally privileged position of the pastor in a religious organization allows him or her to act as a gatekeeper, generating certain beliefs about social issues as well as theological matters; this has been particularly true in American Evangelical Protestantism. The shaping power of the pastor also includes matters of race and gender, and we have seen the display of an implicit, but clear, discourse against interracial unions. Pastors control the physical, and much of the social, space in which both generalized and specific couples can be defined as interracial, legitimate, and acceptable. At Downtown Church, the pastoral leadership manages diversity in subtle and not so subtle ways within the organization, including interracial partnerships. Influenced by their consumption of the city and their need to fit into the diverse cityscape, the racialized urban imaginary of church leaders provides a framework for the ways in which diversity works, where it works, and how to manage it to maximize returns. In addition, opposition to interracial relationships, whether subtle or explicit, aligns with a long cultural history in which the construction of racial differences portrays them as absolute and views romantic partnerships as monoracial (Frankenberg 1993:103).

When imagining the racial other within an urban-based congregation, white leaders carve out a specific space that racial minorities—particularly black men and women—can occupy. As we have seen, this includes visibility, but little direct organizational power or authority. It does not include romantic partnering with white congregants. With Linda and Evan, white church leaders were firm in creating distance (physically and discursively) from potential black partners. The pastor's racialized urban imaginaries were manifest in gendered ways—in both cases the pastors spoke directly to the woman, whether questioning Linda, who is white, directly, or physically escorting me, a multiracial woman, into another conversation. Nonetheless, both actions reinforce an overall protection of whiteness in this diverse religious organization.

It is striking how much the pastors feel it is within their domain of authority to speak about, assess, and directly comment upon the dating lives of their congregants; and they do so in very racialized and gendered ways, whether they recognize that or not. What makes these displays of intervention and authority particularly noteworthy is that it does not happen regularly in the same way in other areas of religious life. None of the cases recounted here were examples of laity inviting the pastor's wisdom, or wanting him to "speak into their lives." As we have seen, congregants were often quite taken aback and upset, even finding this a violation of privacy. Both staff and congregants accept that dating is good and should occur, and even find it natural that it should occur within the church. But there are clear differences among many in their views on internal boundaries. These tensions reveal historical views on protecting whiteness while enacting white masculine power. These historical threads are woven into conservative religious models of dating and marriage in which the spiritual leader possesses a form of authority to shape the private romantic lives of the congregants.

An additional thread throughout the stories is the strong reaction to the coupling of black and white members specifically. Many studies have found that white congregants differentiate between an interracial relationship involving a black person, which is much less acceptable, than one with a Latinx or Asian partner (Perry 2013). This is evident when James referenced the pastors' approval of a white man dating an Asian woman, and in contrast to the discouragement toward black men dating white women. As Rockquemore and Brunsma (2001: ix) argue, "blacks and whites continue to be the two groups with the greatest social distance, the most spatial separation, and the strongest taboos against interracial marriage." Undoubtedly these sentiments contribute to the structural and institutional realities that shape the everyday social interaction between groups, including religious organizations. There are clear consistencies with the long-held notions that emphasize the preservation of white womanhood and the accompanying threat of black masculinity. It is striking that this is still apparent in a religious space where blackness is on display as a positive attraction for enticing what are essentially new consumers. The pastors do not say directly that they disapprove of interracial, especially black-white, partnerships, and, consistent with the idea of color-blind racism, this provides them with the opportunity to deny or explain away their actions.

Ambivalence and Community: Reimagining Inclusivity

Congregations can be great places to meet a significant other. Downtown Church is no different, and perhaps is better than most. It is a church where singles abound, and are indeed the target demographic. Members of Downtown Church find themselves in a city that is full of young, single, like-minded people. Dilemmas of sorting through large numbers of potential partners, or conversely, finding a social setting that caters to people most likely to be similarly attracted, are surely part of what is a significant drawing card for the congregation. Most congregants describe the church generally and DC specifically as a place where relationships happen, a place where they can meet people, "do life together," and share life experiences. One such experience is romantic partnership. Yet congregants find that only certain types of romantic partnerships are supported within the congregation. This creates opportunities for resistance but also sites for hurt and isolation.

As critical race theorists argue, "our social world, with its rules, practices and assignments of prestige and power, is not fixed; rather, we construct it with words, stories and silence" (Delgado and Stefancic 1995:xvii). The racialized urban imaginary of church officials constructs a social world in a way that privileges same-race coupling over other connections at Downtown Church. Couples that choose to operate outside of that normative frame are met with a lack of institutional support, and some are forced to the margins of the organization.

In the cases of Evan and James, we saw that it is difficult for members to make sense of the racialized sentiments the pastoral staff expresses. Interracial coupling seems to bring forth particular racialized attitudes and principles that are otherwise not conveyed publicly within the congregation. But many congregants convey a racialized urban imaginary that sees interracial unions as common, attainable, and desirable in an urban setting. Thus, congregants find ways to explain the pastoral staff's incongruent approach to these types of romantic unions. It is in their ambivalence that we find the ways congregants push back against the dominant narratives regarding intimate partnering. Ambivalence is a tactic enacted in an environment that only consumes diversity but does not embrace it. In order to explain certain outcomes, ambiguity is used as a mechanism for resistance. It allows for congregants to assert their approval of interracial unions without publicly ridiculing the pastoral authority. In some ways, ambivalence also allows for the continued access to community within the church, albeit some members experience this community outside of church walls. Cross-racial community-building is important to congregants who otherwise experience a racially segregated city.

The focus on discursive techniques is important to interrogate, as racial attitudes and practices are not independent of the societal context in which they are embedded, but instead reflect social-structural relations between racial groups. Interracial intimacy is part of a larger story of racial difference. This story of difference is accompanied by many discursive techniques, such as calling a biracial child a swirl baby, that maintain the idea of mutually exclusive social worlds. As Eduardo Bonilla-Silva (1997) claims, racialized discourses and ideologies are fundamentally and recursively connected to racialized social structures. Bonilla-Silva, as well as other contemporary race scholars, have documented how racial discourses and ideologies in the post–civil rights era function to obscure the structural realities of racism and racial inequality, thereby perpetuating racial inequality while simultaneously asserting a message of equality and democracy. Thus, racial ideologies, and the discursive tactics that perpetuate them, play a central, though often covert, role in justifying structural arrangements of racial inequality and providing a logic, or an "organizational map," that assists in the perpetuation of racially oppressive social systems and institutions. Members of Downtown Church are folded into a narrative of diversity consumption, within a religious context, as a justifiable way to traverse racial boundaries. But the pastor's authority within the church privileges certain notions of and limits to racial difference, with significant impact on the public and private lives of the congregants.

While congregants may not like the approach of the pastoral staff, they negotiate ways of operating in this space, with the impact that implies. For members, their discursive tactics are a way to build and maintain community in the face of this intersection of race and power.

Congregants must negotiate between the dominant narratives and what they accept as their reality. As Irby (2013:191) states, "While relationships are a deeply personal practice that involve forming an intimate connection with another person, how people form relationships and make sense of them reveals a significant amount about the social institutions individuals are embedded within." The interracial relationships we see at Downtown Church struggle to challenge racial boundaries. Congregants negotiate the meaning of community, identity, and inclusion within the borders of racial interactions inside the congregation. They may be secretive, they may create communities outside the church with other church members, they may leave the congregation. But it is noteworthy how many do in fact stay in the congregation. Why do people stay in a congregation, when often they disagree with the pastors' practices or find the dominant cultural practices of the church objectionable? What is in it for them to engage in the work of circumventing, or resisting, the pastoral vision and church practices? It is to those questions we now turn.

6

"Should I Stay or Should I Go?"

They need us. They [the pastoral staff] need people who are from the city to help them navigate. They are suburban church kids who don't know the city. It's changing them. They are about fashion and looks, but our city is in need and they have the platform. They have the money and the resources that we don't have. They were able to go into my old school and help and I have been trying to get in there for years. Yeah, they are white but they have the ear of the alderman, so we need to stay and help them and direct them where the real need is. They aren't from here so they really don't know, but they have the heart and I can work with that.
—Larry, black congregant

In this quote from Larry summing up dynamics discussed earlier, we see evidence of tensions between "city" and "suburb" as places and identities. We see tensions between the white leadership and members who are ethno-racial minorities. We see the widespread perception that Downtown Church has an emphasis on looks, fashion, and consumption. But this quote also offers a key to understanding why many people stay in the church despite the tensions. We see both critique and commitment.

Understanding why people first choose a congregation to attend, and why they then stay long enough to have a real commitment and be considered "members," are serious questions for congregations themselves. There are also reasons why these questions might be particularly pertinent to ask about Downtown Church. It is a young church, with some married members but few children, so there is not a long tradition of families as members—no one was raised in this church. Congregants' loyalties cannot be more than a few years old, by definition. And Downtown Church is focusing particularly on the unchurched, trying to appeal to people without church homes, people who are more likely to need to make conscious decisions to attend, as it is less a part of their inherited personal identity. Any study of a religious congregation, particularly a study of a newer congregation that has a less traditional approach to recruiting and growing the membership, will have to engage obvious questions as to what draws potential members, how they experience their new church home, and then why they stay.

Moreover, Downtown Church as a setting raises these questions about staying for other reasons. As we have seen, at various times Downtown Church events have embarrassed some members. There have been interpersonal encounters with the pastoral leadership that have caused awkwardness over racial insensitivity. And there have been several episodes that have just barely skirted issues of what might be considered inappropriate materialism and objectifying women. We have seen examples of people leaving DC after particularly awkward incidents—such as Crystal, who challenged the pastor on incorporating inclusive music, or Grant and Lydia, an interracial couple who did not return after their new child was presented to the congregation as a "swirl baby." Particularly for a congregation in the evangelical Protestant tradition, which is often noted for its social conservatism—as well as, we have noted, its religious innovations in terms of delivering its message through technology and the like—there were many instances at Downtown Church which prompted us to ask the question, "why are people staying with this congregation?" And in particular, "why are people of color staying?"

It's Personal: Reasons for Staying in Downtown Church

The responses to questions about why people liked DC and why they stayed were varied among the members interviewed. Many members appreciated the friendliness, the relaxed casual approach to worship, and the fact that they find the worship services and the congregation entertaining and fun. For example, after a worship service, I heard a group of members discussing that they did not believe they were experiencing the personal spiritual growth they hoped for. I asked one member why she continued to attend if she wasn't getting anything spiritual out of it. She responded, "To be entertained [laughter], for real. I don't know. I asked myself that question the other day. I mean, it's cool, something to do on Sunday. It's like an extension of the weekend."

Connected to that sense of personal enjoyment, a number of members remarked about how "un-churchlike" DC presents itself to be. Christopher, a white member, shares, "I think our generation growing up is tired of, of religion. I think a lot of people may see religion and think that's Christianity." In contrast, Downtown Church's approach seems less like "religion" and more like a truer version of what Christopher hopes Christianity should be. As Melanie, a black woman said,

> Develop those relationships. Make church fun. Make it, you know, don't make it so taboo, but save lives. They [DC staff and founding members] felt that they could be those young people to break that taboo. To break that stigma. And to just you know, let 'em know like, "yeah, I'm young but I'm hip. I love God. I love people. And you don't have to sacrifice a fun-filled life." You know, just to have a relationship with God. You can have both.

Other members put some more specific meaning on the idea of "fun" by explaining how welcoming and friendly the entire church atmosphere is. For example, Timothy, a white man, remarked:

> I had been to some other churches, and of all of the churches I visited in Chicago maybe one or two somebody genuinely said "hi" and wanted to find out about me and what I was doing there, you know. But, Downtown Church I mean, that's, that's really what hooked me, you know. Because people are interested in, you know, me. Why I'm here and what I do.

This response risks sounding quite self-centered—Timothy likes Downtown Church because people are interested in him. But such a welcoming atmosphere should not be dismissed. Sociological research has shown for some time (e.g., Olson 1989, 2008) that the more tightly knit the existing membership is in terms of friendships, the more difficult it can be for newcomers to feel welcome or to find a place to belong. A fairly young church, with a mission dedicated to attracting people without ingrained church backgrounds and who are perhaps new to the city without a real friendship network, is well positioned to use such friendliness to build its membership. It can give these newcomers a sense of belonging.

Another version of this explanation came from Christopher, a white man, who reflected:

> I've gone to church with [my ex-girlfriend] a few times and it just felt very routine, like the preacher would say a certain word and the whole congregation would say something, like an answer to a prayer or they would all pray the same exact prayer at the same time and it was like, I didn't know those things, I was never told what to say there, so I feel, probably, like a little left out you know like, I don't know or maybe I don't belong.

Here Christopher is making two different but intertwined observations. He is expressing a clear preference for a less structured and less liturgical form of worship. Rather than a service built on ritual, often handed down through church traditions over the decades or centuries, he likes a worship service that feels more casual, relaxed, perhaps even spontaneous. He felt uncomfortable in liturgical settings because he didn't know the ritual forms or understand their meanings. He felt left out, and implicitly not welcomed. But beyond that, by noting that it seemed "routine," he seems to be assessing the authenticity and emotions behind the actions. Thus, in two ways Christopher did feel better about Downtown Church—he didn't feel as much like an outsider who didn't know things, and the service itself seemed more genuine and appealing. The ways in which the leadership presents DC as a different type of church experience clearly worked for Christopher.

In a related manner, but around different issues, Marley, a black woman, expressed her approval of Downtown Church:

> [B]ecause when you come in, it's not like, "I don't like your dress blah blah blah blah," that old school stuff, [and] that is awesome. That is what makes me come back a second time, but I still need someone to have a relationship with me.

Marley plays on a consistent image of churches and churchgoers in American culture—that there is too much emphasis on who you are, what you look like and dress like, and that church circles can be especially prone to gossip. So, even though many congregants remarked upon the emphasis put on fashion and good looks within Downtown

Church, Marley feels freed from the "old school stuff" of judgment and personal criticism.

However, at the end of Marley's comment she notes that she still needs "someone to have a relationship with me." This point leads to a consideration of another area into which many responses to "why do you stay" can be grouped—personal benefits that come from being connected to others in the congregation. These are still personal benefits, but they are only obtainable within the context of being with others in the church. For example, several people mentioned the benefit of having the opportunity to gain experience in organizational leadership, or the meaningful relationships they had made with others.

> I keep coming back, I think because of the relationships that I've made. And there's a lot of churches that I could go to I suppose, but nothing's changed as far as me feeling like Downtown Church is the place I'm supposed to be. But, I feel like a lot of that is the relationships. I feel like part of that too is being encouraged, you know, by Pastor Phil or by other people. Having a place to serve you know. And being involved in this ministry.
> —Timothy, white congregant

Several themes are apparent in this quote. Timothy recognizes the many options available for someone seeking a church in an urban center like Chicago. He recognizes a dimension of choice and that he is the one who makes that decision. And yet, DC is the place he is "supposed to be." There is more involved than just his personal preferences. Certainly he recognizes benefits for him—a place to serve, and to be involved in the ministry. He is clearly bolstered by the encouragement he gets from others and the staff. But it isn't just personal. There are relationships, with others, with the congregation, with the leadership, with the ministry and its goals in the city.

James, a black man who is often at DC and worked as a greeter and in other capacities, also made several of these points. When asked why he keeps coming back he responded, "well, I've learned from them. I get challenged from going there on a spiritual level. On a personal level . . ." he trailed off. Knowing that James has been critical of the church leadership on some issues, I asked whether that "challenge" is keeping on, even through those criticisms.

> [I'm getting] something from the message and just the experience of being in a church leadership environment. [This] was the first time I've ever been in that [a place where he is both critical and committed], so it was something new and challenging. But the message has definitely gotten better. And uh, I've developed some friends there. I get to see my friends, as shallow as it may sound but [chuckles]."

While James might be a bit self-conscious about using the church just for a social life, others spoke with great sincerity about the relationships they had formed at DC. Christopher repeatedly talked about the importance of "people" and how DC reached out to help "people," prompting me to ask, "were you always a people person? Because I hear you say 'people, people, people', is this something that's happened while you were at Downtown Church?" Christopher laughed and responded:

> Yeah, I think my eyes were opened to it at Downtown Church. I would say I'm pretty, like I guess it depends on, I'm pretty shy for the most part, and uh, quiet. But I feel like I could be more outgoing with people. I think Downtown Church kind of like allowed me to do that, you know, not, not be so reserved and quiet.

Christopher went on to discuss the centrality of building relationships to the success of the congregation and to the essential religious ministry of the group:

> I don't think, like, all the healing and all the prayer, and all we have as Christians, happens [only] on Sunday. It happens during the week, so . . . you know, if someone comes to Downtown Church, I make it my priority to reach out to them, you know, take them out to lunch, get to know them and just get to know them as a person, and love them. It's not about "you have to do this" or "you have to do that" if you want to come here, it's just building relationships with people.

Linda, who is in an important position as program coordinator for the Overland High School outreach program, echoed many of these thoughts:

> I truly believe that relationships do keep people. So there are key relationships, whether you have a relationship with the key leader or not. I mean, if I'm going to leave Downtown Church, then I'm not going to be seeing Vanessa two or three times a week like I do. And some of my relationships with my team members are more like acquaintance relationships. But, I know them more intimately because of, you know; I kind of just have to know what's going on with them. Uh, so [leaving would be] kind of breaking that. I don't wanna let anybody down. And then, uh, other people, who may not have relationships with key leaders, do have relationships with one another. And are still seeking stuff out for themselves.

The relationships formed within the congregation are personally fulfilling for many, and spiritually and socially important for others. They are social, but also religiously meaningful.

Community and Calling

Other respondents gave answers less oriented to their personal satisfaction and growth, but instead marked by a sense of calling—both to a religious duty and to a community. Sometimes that community was the Downtown Church congregation itself, and elements of that are evident in several of the quotations above. Community, for many people, was important personally but also about the religious purpose of a church and of Christian identity. It is not something that one just chooses to do or not to do; it has a normative quality that puts it at the center of being in a church.

When James had finished his comment about friendships with a sheepish laugh and indicated it might be "shallow" to go to church just for the social part, I responded, "Actually I bet a lot of people come to see their friends." James agreed, "Yeah. I've heard that too, a lot. So yeah." But he went on with a significant re-direction:

> I honestly feel like God is keeping me there for some reason and it may be because of those things that I end up seeing, and other people that might

see that I'm still there for them, because if they don't know how to then they'll never know. If you're just like, "I'll just back off 'cause I don't like that, I'm not going to stay there." So it's just kinda like looking back on the series of events that just led up to me being there [DC]. From coming back home, not going to church with my parents, starting at his [Pastor Phil's] father's church, as soon as my schedule changed; Phil was starting church in the city. So it's just kind of the series of events, just wound up like, "ok, well . . ."

James is laying out several layers of ideas about commitment. There are friendships and social relationships. But he stays despite issues with the leadership staff, or particular events, because he has a calling and a duty. If he is not there, if he withdraws just because of his own dissatisfaction, he says, others will miss his witness. Others will miss the truth behind the stumbles, and "they'll never know" what the church and the message could hold for them. He then recounts a long string of events, with the clear implication that they were not random, but rather were ordered with the purpose of getting him to this place and at this time. Events in his personal life landed him in the Big Church run by Pastor Phil's father, and just as Downtown Church was being planted in the city, James's schedule changed to allow him to be there. Now that he is, his sense of responsibility to the congregation and those in it overrides any personal discomfort.

Marley, a black woman who often volunteers, also portrays her being at Downtown Church as a calling—it is bigger than her, but it has been ideally situated to allow her to use her gifts:

> I would say number one, I primarily felt led to continue with Downtown Church and support Downtown Church and be planted at Downtown Church. But I also felt like in addition to feeling led by God to do that, I also felt like this is a place where things that I brought, as being long term, you know, everybody was seeming new and starting a church. I had a long-term history with church and thought that could be helpful.

Far from being "unchurched," Marley had numerous experiences with and skills in church work and thought DC would allow her to use them. She sees God's hand behind her path, and thus takes seriously the idea that she belongs and has an obligation to help others find their way. She continued:

> So, I just, you know, I was there and invited a couple of people, and kept praying about "God, is this where you want me to be?" And I think I just really, you know, as I said, I was thinking like, "I have done this for so long and all of these young people I believe they're growing in their relationship with Christ. Their faith is growing and I'm still taught." But, here's a place that perhaps could use what gifts God has given me and maybe to help build it. And so I would say number one, I primarily felt led to continue with Downtown Church and support Downtown Church and be planted at Downtown Church.

This language of calling is not the vocabulary of "choosing" and "church shopping" that some theories of church participation feature as the heart of membership and commitment. This discourse may be about the self, in that those using it feel a personal responsibility to use what they perceive as God's gifts. But it is about the self in deep relations with others—and deeply bound by a sense of religious duty, and an opportunity, that is only partly under their control. People feel that they have a purpose with their faith and with their participation, and the specific church in which this happens is to be understood in all its complexity and contradiction as being part of that plan.

Dylan, a black woman, voiced similar themes—both about her frustrations and about her commitment:

> If I didn't commit to staying I would have left already. I wouldn't be here. But there is something here. There is no way that, by accident, all these young people who are from all different areas are coming here. [Pastor] Phil is from an influential family and his heart led him here. We [Downtown Church] are just in a wilderness period. When you have a bunch of leaders who aren't ready to mentor or be mentored, we are going to wander around a bit. But Chicago needs this. This city is so divided so it needs a group like this. I don't know if the leadership grasps that, and that is also the disconnect. When I talk about they really want to be the hands and feet of God, it's the leadership, it is really the leadership, they have a heart for that, they honestly do. It is just

their human side that kind of gets a little funky, but that I mean, you can say the same thing about me.

Dylan is clearly not ignoring the missteps by the pastors, or the sense that the pastoral leadership is in unfamiliar waters trying to navigate a new church planted in the middle of the city. But she sees this challenge as requiring a need for mentoring and guidance, not as a reason to leave—even if it may well have occurred to her. She wants to extend some understanding and forgiveness to others as she would like to have extended to her, but more than that, she sees herself in a position of duty and opportunity. What is particularly interesting is her conviction that Chicago—as a city—needs some of the things that Downtown Church has to offer. Dylan knows how distinct it is, in a hyper-segregated city like Chicago, to have people from different areas of the city come together and build relationships. She is committed as she believes the church requires the efforts of people like her so that it can respond to the city's needs.

Interestingly, the idea that the community of focus was Chicago, as a city, came up in several interviews and informal conversations. Others besides Dylan felt that Chicago "needed" a church like Downtown Church. They understood the city as a particular social and geographical space that required a particular type of religious organization to meet its needs. Paula, a white woman, remarked, "I do believe what [Pastor Phil] says about always having a heart for the city and loving the city. And, um . . . that God is calling him to the city obviously, because he's been given great favor to this point, here in the city."

The potential importance of Downtown Church to Chicago came up in several peoples' comments. More than once (and not just from the pastors) we heard that Chicago was one of the most "unchurched" cities in the United States, and thus a church designed particularly to reach out to the unchurched was well-positioned to grow, but also would fulfill a real social need. Similarly, we heard several people recount as "fact" that Chicago is one of the youngest cities in the country and again, a church aimed at young people was thus important. Regardless of the statistical merit of that claim, Chicago's population profile is less significant than the importance that the pastoral staff and the membership place on those ideas, and the underlying message—that Chicago needs

Downtown Church, that it has enormous opportunity to grow, and the potential to serve as a vital good to the community. Chad, who is involved in leading the music ministry, sums up this sentiment:

> I mean we're, I think we're a city that is very diverse, very young, and I think like right now you just look at our potential, what it is we can become and we're on an international stage, you know, and an international city, so I think, I think, there's just a lot of room to grow.

But the idea that Downtown Church is a church for the city, and for Chicago specifically, is more than just that it is well-suited to the niche of its target demographic and thus can be an organizational success story. Again, Chad reiterates sentiments shared by many that the diversity and youth of the church are vital to reaching a young, racially divided city. Furthermore, many see Chicago as having particular need for moral and spiritual witness. Melanie, vocalist on the worship team, said:

> I think [the leaders] feel like it's their mission to take back the city. Because, I mean, I don't know specifically, but I know that they've constantly said, that statistics shows that Chicago is like the biggest city that's the most, I don't wanna say sinful, but in a way yes. And in the same sense that it's a big city with lots of churches, but no one's committed to their churches like here. Everyone is still very young, and I think for, Pastor Phil and Pastor Paul, you know, they feel like it's their mission to take back the city. And to bring God back to the city. Because it's not there. He's not there. I think he said one time that there were literally twice as many liquor stores in the city than there are churches.

This notion resonates with the long tradition in evangelical Protestantism of seeing the city as a site of sin and social problems. Melanie remains with DC because she is moved by the insight into perceived social ills on the part of the pastoral staff and their commitment to rectifying them. Other members included aspects of inequality as one of those social problems. They see Chicago as a particularly segregated city, with deep racial divisions that, along with economic inequality, threaten to tear the municipal fabric irreparably. Kyle, long-time member and former volunteer, commented,

Sometimes I feel like it's kind of a segregated city in some ways, like there's different areas and neighborhoods that have like one race or something. [The point of] Downtown Church is to make it not feel like a church and break all the rules and expectations of what a church is, because if you read the Bible, the church is just a body of people, you know, it's not a building, it's not a race, it's not an age group—it's just people that share that faith and that belief.

Thus, Downtown Church can help transcend social differences and even address social conflict with a version of the faith that can be truly shared. Reaching out to the unchurched is important to that mission, especially the young and unchurched in the city. As Larry indicated earlier, this can have a more practical dimension of putting faith into social action—Downtown Church has its problems, but it has resources and stature that have given him and others the opportunity to work for social healing in places they had not been able to before.

Yet, not everyone is convinced. As Valerie, the only Chicago resident on the Elder Board, noted earlier, she thought folks from Indiana misunderstood Chicago, relying on stereotypes and glamorized images of city. Valerie remains a member even despite the shallow representation of "her city" on behalf of the pastoral staff. She is willing to stay with Downtown Church and try to provide the much needed guidance and support she suggests. She offers key insights into the vantage point of the church leadership staff to address what may have contributed to their mishaps. However, Valerie comments on their shortsightedness while remaining a committed member of the board. She seems to believe that they have an important and positive potential, so the gaffes and stumbles are just that—steps on the way to doing something important for the city, to which she seems very devoted. As noted previously, even when the congregational leadership fails to appreciate the situation in the city, or the lives of African Americans and the challenges they face—and even when they are uneven with their follow-through—many in the congregation find a way to put themselves in a situation to do something they can feel good about. Larry clearly sees a trade-off and is not blind to the costs of the leadership's mistakes. But he carries on, because he also has opportunities there that he has not had before.

Downtown Church emphasizes diversity in its congregation and is proud of the fact that it has whites, blacks, Asians, and Latinx sitting in the pews together, even if they are not always explicit about what "diversity" means in practical terms. That vision is also undercut by the ideology and practices of managed diversity, and an instrumental approach to the racial utility of black bodies that intentionally or not reproduces the exoticizing and othering of those on the margins of the American racial order. But the idea of potentially being able to participate in creating a truly "rainbow church" (in Sonja's terms) inspired a number of people. They voiced frustrations with several programming efforts within the church, they often disagreed deeply—if privately—with Pastor Phil and the church leadership—but they felt they had a calling to stay with it, to take advantage of the positive things that they could, and be a part of something larger than themselves.

This commitment became apparent among the interracial "outlaws"—the interracial couples who kept their romantic relationships secret in church but met in various places to socialize. Despite this marginalization in the congregation, their position on the outskirts of the group seemed to spark a deeper sense of dedication to the church. Kelly and Rich, who were celebrating six months together on the evening I was introduced to the group, saw the potential for a "rainbow church." They believed their continued presence at the church would help that effort along. Kelly said, "If we leave, then how will the church grow?" For Kelly, her compliance with, or secretive resistance to, the church's racial dynamics resulted in a greater sense of commitment for the greater good of the religious community and the city. Indeed, Kelly expressed a sense of authority and a responsibility to enact a vision of the church without the church's pastoral staff actually knowing about it. In effect, she was using the church's goals and vision in her own way, quietly usurping the pastor's authority. Her own imaginary of the city, and of its racial order, gave DC the potential to be a space unlike any other in the city—a space she has the power to help create.

However, this is not solely instrumental behavior on Kelly's part, with her acting openly compliant only as a means to gain the opportunity to achieve her ends. Orit Avishai (2008) found that women in conservative religious traditions do not engage in submission only to seek instrumental ends, but their actions represent a form of modified empowerment or resistance. Rather, Avishai suggests that people are compliant with religious structures because they are invested in the religious outcomes and goals of the community. They may adhere to church strictures because even if they feel personally ambivalent about it, doing so becomes part of being in the community and enacting their faith. Adapting that argument here can help to explain why individuals remain dedicated to this religious community that is at times racially oppressive.

While the pastors promote racial inclusivity in particular ways, the discourse and context create the possibility and rationale for people to reinterpret the pastors' "official" vision. The "outlaw" couples, for example, are taking part of the message of the church and extending it into areas with which the leadership doesn't feel comfortable. Because that area is the members' own personal relationships, however, they can do it outside of the physical space of the church even as they still maintain a commitment to participate fully in the church.

Yet many of the outlaw couples, such as Kelly and Rich, both serve as leadership on volunteer teams but are not publicly "out" as an interracial couple. Remaining hidden reconstructs in many ways the very structures of stigma the couple is trying to break down. And by keeping their relationship "on the DL" ("down low") these couples suffer some personal consequences. They are rendered invisible. Important elements of their own lives are downplayed—intimate relationships and their own sense of faith. In these circumstances, they "do" religion (Avishai 2008) by following along with the public vision of the community but with ambivalence and hesitation and hurt.

Staying Downtown

A consistent question for those who found and lead churches is "what draws people to a specific church?" and, once there, "what keeps people coming to that church?" In part, this is a follow-up to the question of why people go to church at all, and sociological research has found two basic sets of answers. First, religion provides a meaning system that offers adherents ways to understand their lives and their purposes, including morals, values, and ethics for living in society. Religion organizes human relationships with the divine as well as with each other. Second, religion can provide community to people, with a sense of belonging, social and emotional support networks, and practical aid and relationships. Humans are social creatures, and religion combines living with other people with a sense of higher purpose and rules to facilitate that living.

But those considerations do not answer why people choose any specific faith or religious community, a crucial question for those who run such organizations. Why choose this one over another? Of course, many people don't really choose their religious community in any particularly meaningful way. They are raised in one religious tradition, come to understand themselves and their identity as thoroughly enmeshed in that tradition, and cannot imagine themselves in any other religion. Both the dimensions of meaning and belonging are fully satisfied for them where they are. Others, who make a more conscious choice about joining a particular church, then must find reasons to stay in it.

These questions of commitment are particularly pertinent in the contemporary United States, where religion is "disestablished" from government and thus the power of the state cannot force one to believe, to attend, or to support a religious organization. Further, given that there is no officially state-sanctioned religion, those religious communities that do exist must rely on the voluntary efforts and support of their members. Religious organizations, in a sense, must "compete" for their members. People are free to come and go, seeking to find the community and beliefs that best suit their lives. A culture of voluntarism dominates the way most Americans think of religion, and over time the assumption has grown that only voluntary, freely chosen, religious commitments are truly authentic.

These dynamics are even more salient in urban centers. More people, arriving from a variety of different places, bring a variety of religious practices and beliefs with them. Cities are places of intense religious innovation (e.g., Orsi 1999; Williams 2002) with new hybrid faiths emerging, and already established groups changed by new members, or experiencing schisms and division into multiple groups. When members of a religious community have contact with members of different communities every day, they cannot remain unchanged. They may attempt to retreat further into themselves, to fend off contact with others, or they may be open to new ideas, people, and practices (Williams 2006). But urban religion has a history in the United States of being the place where the competition for members is greatest, and the options for potential members are the most varied. Thus, questions of "why this church" and "why stay" become particularly relevant for this book and for Downtown Church itself.

"Church" in Black and White

Not surprisingly, while there was a variety of responses to queries about staying that ranged across many different congregants, and many people used several different explanations, there was a noticeable clustering of responses among white and black church members. White members were, in general, less critical of the pastoral leadership, while black and to some extent Latinx members were more likely to express their commitment in terms of calling and community rather than purely personal benefits. One possible explanation for this pattern is that many white members were relatively new to churchgoing and/or did not have much religious background; on the other hand, many of the black members did have prior experiences with churches and an already developed faith. Thus, they could more naturally use a religiously inflected language of calling, rather than thinking primarily of Downtown Church as just another group or a place to learn such language.

But two considerations make the racial differences in congregants' responses seem connected to more than just prior experience with religion. First is the pattern we have seen of Downtown Church prizing diversity and welcoming people of many ethno-racial backgrounds, while still retaining all serious leadership positions among the circle of white suburbanites who came with Pastor Phil to start Downtown Church. Along with other dynamics—such as the racial utility of placing black members in positions where they are visible-but-not-too-visible, and Pastor Phil's occasional mimicking of a "black" dialect when speaking, or the discouraging of interracial romantic couples—it is not surprising that black members would be more likely to find things to criticize than would white members.

However, more foundationally, we see in Downtown Church an example of a general pattern, which reflects differing ways in which religious commitment is articulated among white and black Americans. Williams, Irby, and Warner (2016) document that among young adults, white college students take a much more "client"-oriented approach to church involvement than do black college students. Both groups of students may have spent time looking at several different congregations while trying to find a comfortable "church home"; that is, they may engage in what scholars often call "church shopping." But the ways in which they articulate their motivations—and what makes a particular congregation an appropriate church home—differ. White college students articulated a sense of their own spiritual needs and personal growth, and they often evaluated congregations or other religious organizations based on how the group helped them achieve those things. They would move in and out of specific groups based on what they needed or what they were finding meaningful. Black students, on the other hand, spoke consistently of community, of a calling, and used "family" metaphors to describe their churches. They spoke less about choosing and more about being called, or having a responsibility.

Christerson, Edwards, and Flory (2010) also found distinct differences in the religious orientations between white and black young people (their study also included Latinx and Asian Americans). They found white young adults to be much more individualistic in their orientations to religion and to religious authority, while black respondents were more loyal to particular churches and faith traditions and more respectful of religious authority, and authorities. As both Williams et al. (2016), and Christerson et al. (2010) conclude, the modern religious individualism and shopping orientation that is thought to be the essence of contemporary American Christianity (e.g., Hammond 1992, or Roof 1999) is much more likely to pertain to white Americans than to African Americans. Partly this is a response to social marginality and often precarious economic statuses—the church as a community can be part of a bulwark against the vagaries of life and risk. Religious groups can provide social, emotional, and even financial support, and form an important social network for coping with misfortune and discrimination.

As Downtown Church works to become a church in the city and for the city, it has reproduced some of these community dynamics—but to the extent that the community of the congregation is more centered on the needs and satisfactions of its white members, the less sure black and other people of color can be that they can find such support there. As we have seen, many of DC's minority members had deep hopes for a multiracial church that could provide societal healing and social leadership, but their commitment was sometimes strained, if not even broken, by the ways in which DC falls short of their hopes. Even so, many continue to find meaningful personal relationships and meaningful spiritual purpose within the congregation. They are not necessarily blind to racialized dynamics, but can see a greater purpose and a longer term than what might be obvious to those looking in from the outside.

By examining Downtown Church from a number of angles, including its organizational founding, its conceptualizations of its market and its brand, and the ways in which these ideas are informed by a racialized urban imaginary that shapes the ways the leadership aims to be a "city church," we have seen how that larger imaginary has helped to foster organizational practices such as the one we termed managed diversity, and how these have often been built on the racial utility of using the embodied presences of minority members and attractive women to help attract and keep members—even as they expressed part of the congregation's corporate identity. The final chapter draws on these observations to consider some of the larger dynamics of religion, race, and place in the United States.

Conclusion

The City Imagined

I think it's hard to define Downtown Church or to even probably really see where Downtown Church is going if you're not close to leadership, 'cause leadership is still trying to figure out where we are and get a stable foundation in the city and a stable foundation in ministry. And so, it's like a baby—one month we may feel like "okay, maybe this is where we are going," but then the next month it's like, okay, maybe that's not quite where we're supposed to go. So we're crawling right now and we're trying to learn to walk.

—Tamiya, black congregant

This book has sought to "place" Downtown Church. It has illuminated the dynamics between its internal organizational workings, its external outreach, and the setting in which it exists. In particular, it has examined the intersections among the cultural understandings and social structures of race, gender, and economic class that are involved with the attempt at founding an urban church. The issues we have examined here, including tensions, conflicts, synergies, hopes and disillusionments, relationships within the congregation, questions of religious and organizational authority, interactions among ethno-racially diverse congregants, and the balance between being "in the world" and being "of the world," are common to white evangelical Protestantism. However, these issues took shape with particular twists resulting from this particular urban setting and how that setting was understood by the people involved. Downtown Church offered an illuminating prism through which to see complicated interactions among religion, race, gender, the city, and cultural consumption.

This book has shed light on the various ways in which the pastoral leadership of DC articulated and worked toward realizing their goals of being a "city church," as well as how church members perceived the congregation and its purposes, and reacted to those dynamics. All of the church's efforts to achieve its goals, and all of the reactions to those efforts by members of the leadership teams and the general congregation, rely upon a set of conceptualizations about what constitutes "the city." One cannot aim to be a church in and for the city without some ideas, often implicit, about what the city is and what it should be.

Varied imaginaries of the city used—again, often implicitly—by different groups within the congregation brought to the forefront cultural imaginings and conceptions of race, urban dwellers, and the urban landscape. These imaginings often rely on stereotypical tropes of authenticity, the incorporation of a white middle-class consumer lifestyle centered on the city, and the racialization of urban space. This racialization is manifested in the deep association of the urban with black people, black culture, and a racial hierarchy built on ethno-racial differences. Turning the lens inward, to focus on the manifestations of the imaginary in organizational practices, revealed what turned out to be precarious orientations to congregational diversity, and the resulting organizational practices surrounding the presence of certain minority groups within the congregation were often fraught with tension. As a result, the diversity thought to be natural to the urban place was nonetheless thought to require "managing" by the leadership. And one of the tools to manage diversity was the "utility" of displaying representatives from different racial groups in ways meant to communicate to both current congregational members and potential members messages that the church is both exciting and safe. These three key concepts, *racialized urban imaginary*, *managed diversity*, and *racial utility* animate the substantive chapters of the book and we discuss each in turn here. We then turn to some thoughts about race, religion, and place that push beyond our specific case, first by thinking about multiracial churches and American life, and then by reflecting on how considerations of social and physical space shape race, gender, and religion more generally.

Racialized Urban Imaginary: Church and the City

Cities are deeply symbolic settings. Often they are seen as symbolic stand-ins for the nation in which they exist—for example, London, Paris, Tokyo. Cities have often been thought about as dangerous, as politically corrupt, and as morally fallen. In the United States there is a deep national narrative that locates the frontier, the wilderness, the small town or rural farm, as that which is quintessentially "American." And this image lingers. The presidential election of 2016 reinforced some of this notion as there was a significant cleavage between urban and rural/small-town voting patterns (Badger, Bui, and Pearce 2016; Gamio 2016), with the party that garnered more of the latter votes often describing their constituents as "real" Americans. At the same time, urban locations are seen as sites of high culture, of mass popular entertainment, and as places where one can reinvent oneself and start a new life. One can get "anything" in a big city and part of their excitement comes through notions of consumption. Particularly among certain social classes, cities are places of sophistication and consumption simultaneously.

This urban imaginary is built deeply into the founding principles of Downtown Church. DC doesn't seek families with small children; it doesn't organize multiple nights of small group ministries for different age groups. The single, early career person, with an eye toward fashion and an appreciation of slickly produced, professionally executed worship services, is the key focus. DC takes full advantage of cultural connotations that come with its location in a rented theater. Pastor Phil and Downtown Church thrive on the notion, "you can be cool and still be a churchgoer." Being boring, or being too conventional, is a bigger sin, than being too concerned with how you look, how you dress, or whether you drink.

The pressure experienced by urban religious leaders in their efforts to gain legitimacy for accomplishing "God's work" in the city—especially reaching out to young adults looking to wed their city life with an exploration of or return to their faith—is not lost on many congregational members. And the leadership's efforts at embodying a true urban aesthetic are often rewarded with some eye-rolling by members who are Chicago city residents, and consider the pastoral staff as too "suburban" to be authentically "Chicago." Even members who are invested in the church, devote many volunteer hours to it, and often hold responsibilities for running church programs, can be critical about the extent to which the church doesn't yet really "get it."

In part, this tension is due to the intricate ways in which diversity is tied into the racialized urban imaginary and the ideas that form about whether Downtown Church is itself authentically urban. For voluntary institutions such as congregations, diversity can be not only an aspiration and moral imperative, but also a competitive standard in the broader American context. Diversity is a market trend—it is hot, current, exciting, also validating, accessible, and, in cities like Chicago, an exclusive opportunity. There is a classed aspect to diversity, as it can connote a certain cosmopolitan and cultured status; in that sense, cultural consumers become patrons who consume and appreciate diversity's contents. Others, of course, then become the "objects" to be consumed.

Multiculturalism, as an ideological approach to pluralism in the United States, has usually been considered to be about race and ethnicity, rather than religion (Williams 2015). But racial and ethnic multiculturalism has a decided impact on how religion is practiced and by whom. Various studies of congregational worship practices, such as those by Mark Chaves (2004) and Korie Edwards (2008), demonstrate that different ethno-religious groups use different worship practices (such as raising of hands to pray, or coming forward to give the monetary offering rather than passing a plate back through the pews). Some of these practices or preferences become associated with particular groups—the best example being gospel music and African American religion (see Marti 2012). Varied religious practices both help form a religious identity for individuals and give a message to others about "what kind" or "whose" congregation this is; it can be a symbol of religious multiculturalism, or it can represent that a particular group within the congregation really controls the church. Once again, the intersection of race and religion works to send potentially contradictory messages simultaneously. And in a geographic setting with a number of alternative places for potential members to find church homes—such as a big city—handling the ambiguity of cultural identity markers is a challenge for any congregation.

As we saw, the association with the city and the notion that the city means diversity inverts traditional evangelical imaginaries of the city. The city becomes a place where opportunity and diversity are happening, and these are positive things rather than sinful. Diverse peoples are to be welcomed into the religious community rather than closing the community to those outside the "chosen." Evangelical churches have worked in urban spaces extensively since the early twentieth century, but usually with a mission of conversion and reform. Cities were mission fields, crying out for redemption and salvation. And there is evidence of that attitude in the frequency with which Downtown Church cites Chicago as a leading "unchurched" city and thus in need of DC in particular. But the congregation's goal seems to imply that DC's approach is not needed because it is particularly moral, or conserving traditional values, or a saving resurrection of that "old-time religion." Rather, DC fits in Chicago because the city is young, hip, dynamic, and diverse—and so is the congregation.

Thus, this is a new imaginary for the city and the urban congregation. DC and churches like it now have the opportunity to play up particular experiences, understand the personal explorations in the life histories of their congregants, and their current life challenges and opportunities. In this approach, churches are imagining cities in a different way, affecting organizational transitions into city centers. As a result, urban evangelical churches are being confronted with a whole host of new cultural outlets, but also cultural challenges. Evangelicalism is not new to the city. But the way Downtown Church views itself as being a part of the city and for the city, and not just trying to morally reform the city, is a more recent development. That the city is being valued and valorized is something new. As congregations continue to think about diversity and to engage with cities in new ways, there is an increasing need for future research in this area.

The racialized urban imaginary that informs the perspective of church leaders constructs a racialized and classed aesthetic that is not altogether native to the city of Chicago, but is invested in by both leaders and members even if there is contestation over the meanings. There is no guarantee that when one arrives in the city itself, one is "authentically Chicago" simply because one lives (or works) within the city limits. In keeping with the fabrication of the urban authentic, even congregational members who are both city residents and represent "diversity" are subject to re-branding. Voluntary organizations are in a market-driven environment where they compete for the time and energy of potential members who can in turn expand their resources (see Finke and Stark 1992; for an explicit consideration of this dynamic in Chicago's African American communities, see Reed 2011). Downtown Church capitalizes on the consumerist economy of Chicago as a post-industrial global city (Bennett 2010), playing with different symbols and cultural projects to aid in manufacturing an authentic urban experience for their target consumer. However, while Downtown Church attempts to incorporate a diverse consumer body into its membership, it implicitly reproduces structures of inequality on the axes of class, gender, and race.

Managed Diversity: Race, Authenticity, and the City

Religious organizations are not immune to the power of race in this country. Race is a central organizing force in the United States (Omi and Winant 1994) and religion, either culturally or as an institution, is no exception to this. Indeed, religion, particularly Christianity, is arguably the most racially segregated institution in the United States, and has a long history of justifying the racial order as part of God's will (e.g., Emerson and Smith 2000). As we saw, relationships between race and place, in conjunction with the need to establish an authentic urban identity, drive the Downtown Church congregation to participate in racially charged practices influenced by the racialization of the urban landscape. Varied and often stilted notions of the city bring to the forefront cultural imaginings and conceptions of race, urban dwellers, and the urban landscape that play a key role within congregations moving to urban centers. The racialization of space is often overlooked in studies focused on racial dynamics within religions settings, but it offers valuable insights into the organizational practices predominantly white religious organizations employ to develop racially diverse congregations, especially in urban areas.

While Chicago is known for its diversity, the cultural association between Chicago and blackness in particular is undeniable. Chicago has been referred to by scholars and historians as the "Black Mecca" and the "Black Metropolis" (e.g., Drake and Cayton 1945). Some of the best known of contemporary black Americans, such as Oprah Winfrey or President Barack Obama and First Lady Michelle Obama, claim Chicago as home. Chicago's role as a destination for black Southerners during the Great Migration was captured by painter Jacob Lawrence and in one of playwright August Wilson's "Century Series" plays. Electrified blues music, represented by artists such as Muddy Waters, Buddy Guy, or Junior Wells, was born in Chicago. Rap artists such as Common, Da Bratt, and Chance the Rapper, rep their Chicago roots as they eloquently craft their bars. And the Nation of Islam, one of the best known manifestations of African American Islam, moved to Chicago shortly after its founding in Detroit and is still headquartered on Chicago's South Side. Thus, a racialized imaginary of Chicago is integrally connected to African Americans.

For leaders and congregants of Downtown Church, urban authenticity is heavily rooted in racial difference and the commodification of urban blackness. Church officials find the presence of black bodies important to legitimate themselves as authentic in this unfamiliar urban space. While these representation schemes fall outside of the conventions of more traditional white evangelical religious institutions, they reflect the unique complexities found in creating a congregation where location is at the center of the church's identity formation (where other churches, for example, might place a denominational identity).

The racial history of cities and their current racial demographics receive little consideration in the discussion surrounding urban sensationalism and urban environments. Urban sensationalism (as well as a tradition in American religion) posits urban cities as spiritually wild but fails to address the place of race in that conversation. Place facilitates a different type of race work than that which has been previously addressed in the analysis of racial dynamics within congregations.

In their efforts to be successful in the urban market, Downtown Church leaders engaged in "managed diversity," shaping new and complex ways of addressing congregational diversity and inclusion. Racial diversity and management was at the forefront of their endeavors and yet never explicitly addressed in a collective setting with the congregation. Race is an active part of shaping the lives of those in the congregation and became central to the church's identity as "not too white" and at the same time "not a black church." Congregants and church leaders brought different baselines of racial meaning to their construction of a church in the city of Chicago—a city marked by residential segregation and systematic oppression that has divided it along racial lines for more than a century. For these reasons, we opted to analyze our findings within the framework of racial formation.

Racial formation allows us to understand the ways in which racial dynamics are explained through a linkage between structure and representation, in order to reorganize resources along particular racial lines. Race is an active and central part of the development and organizational practices of this congregation. Congregants and leaders negotiated back and forth between differing racial realities, all in an effort to gain members and create a religious environment that they believe is unmatched in the city. Church leaders in many ways are not attempting to preserve the status quo in comparison to other churches that are "all white," but nonetheless implicitly recreated racial hierarchies and inequitable systems in the process. While race was seldom if ever mentioned in a corporate setting, it was consistently talked about and negotiated on the ground. Leaders and congregants are not denying race but in some ways intentionally seeking it out due to their placement in the city. Church leaders and congregants experience Chicago as a racially diverse space and expect their congregation to be no different. However, the pastoral leadership in particular feels the necessity to curate their congregation in such a way that it "comfortably" balances the presence of its black members within worship services, outreach programs, and congregational authority structures. The complicated ways in which church officials and members interact with race shift the discussion toward understanding race as a commodity and recognizing racial appropriation, all in the pursuit of diversity and authenticity in the city.

The city of Chicago, its rich history, and its racial legacy prompt church leaders and congregants to engage in race management (explicitly or not), ultimately in ways that replicate the stigmatization of blackness while praising the presence of other racial groups. Intentionally or not, blackness is a "problem" to be solved in the congregation. While there is some social value in blackness in social and cultural exchanges within the church, pastoral leaders recognize the reality that whites may flee a setting with too many black folks present. And stereotypes about black men that see them as imposing, dangerous, and too "street" are unintentionally reinforced when the number and appearance of black men are regulated. They act as greeters, but only those with a particular look. They play music in the worship service, but do not direct the band or the music ministry. They are closely monitored as being appropriate romantic partners for only some of the congregation's women. And they are kept out of budgeting authority. At the same time, those stereotypes are used when DC puts together a basketball team to play in a city recreational league. In this way, we find Downtown Church participates in a racialized culture of commodity and consumption. Downtown Church manages diversity to achieve its goals in the competitive urban church market that involves a constant tug and pull between commodification and racial appropriation. Congregational leaders are careful not to appropriate black church culture too much (for example, most of the music remains within the white Evangelical tradition and clothing dress codes are hip, but not Afro-centric) even while consuming some African American cultural forms. However, there is an intimacy with appropriation that is not fully present in the church. Rather, church leaders put much effort into consuming urbanicity and blackness by managing it at arm's length. Managing diversity reminds us of the enduring construction of urban blackness within contemporary constructions of diversity in the American city.

Racial Utility: Diversity, Inclusion, and Who Is Using Whom?

As this book has argued, managed diversity encompasses a number of activities that occur within the congregation for the purpose of balancing the goals of diversity, and authenticity, with the social reality and social perceptions of a city like Chicago. The Downtown Church staff desires a congregation in which diversity is in balance, with no particular ethno-racial group over-represented and—crucially—the white leadership drawn from the home church unchallenged. Thus, managed diversity is a goal, as well as a process. And it is a goal that is largely about the congregation's self-identity, although it is clear that one of the reasons that the pastoral staff is concerned about it is that they are acutely aware of the potential that church image has to attract or rebuff new members.

Our third key concept, "racial utility," is also an organizational practice, but in ways more oriented toward audiences external to the congregation rather than an internal congregational concern. Racial utility is the calculation and strategic thinking that goes into the use and display of racial identity in order to achieve particular ends. For example, a select number of African American men are consistently used as greeters—people who welcome congregants when they arrive for worship services. That black men are at the church's front door is clearly a part of DC's attempt to present itself as "diverse." Greeters tend to be good-looking and dress fashionably—another way in which DC advertises itself as a church for the city's young, single, cosmopolites. Further, church members who are members of various ethno-racial minorities also serve in visible roles on some of the volunteer teams that do much of the practical running of the congregation.

This book has not argued that members of minority groups should not have positions of visibility within the congregation. Quite the contrary, we note that often these positions of great visibility are *not* accompanied by structural organizational authority and leadership. The creative and leadership teams are paid positions, they remain overwhelmingly white and overwhelmingly staffed by people who first became associated with the Big Church in Indiana, then moved to the Downtown Church plant. Volunteer teams are often quite diverse, but they are volunteers and serve at the behest of the pastoral staff. They are, in fact, managed. Indeed, as we saw, several members expressed some frustration at not getting the opportunity to move into real leadership positions, despite their commitment to the church.

Along with paid organizational authority, another limit on thorough inclusion of diverse racial groups emerges in the dynamics surrounding interracial romantic relationships. A number of members of the church who are quite visible in the congregation, and treated as key to congregational success by Pastor Phil and staff, feel as though they are discouraged from dating interracially. Their utility as signs of successful diversity and inclusion seems to end at the point where their personal lives do not align with the racialized imaginary of the staff. The significant example of one couple—who dated, married, and had a child without letting anyone in church leadership know—is instructive. While Pastor Phil publicly expressed great enthusiasm for their relationship and child when they first came back to Sunday worship, there was a strain in the interaction that many saw as masking Phil's disapproval. The couple was embarrassed at the public presentation of their child during the service—a presentation that ostentatiously called attention to their interracial union rather than celebrating their happiness. They did not return to the church after that.

Racial utility can work in both directions. Downtown Church's involvement in a city basketball league was a clear case of racial utility. Pastor Phil assembled a team made up of several of DC's black members, and recruited a couple of their friends, in order to present the church as truly of the city. A local African American high school principal, at a school where DC was starting an outreach program, also played on the team, a clear attempt at ingratiating the church and its agenda with local political power. The usefulness of the black members to the church leadership's public agenda was clear. At the same time, several of the men on the basketball team were also using Pastor Phil's whiteness, and the resources that came from the Big Church, for their own ends. Larry, in particular, was quite cognizant that he was being used in a way to establish DC's credibility with the city and the neighborhood. Yet he noted that he had never been able to get into the local high school with any other service-provision program. Downtown Church, with its white leadership and deep pockets, was able to set up an outreach program into the high school. Larry wanted to be there; racial utility was the price of making that happen and it was useful in both directions. It was not an equal exchange, as a power dynamic between the white middle-class and black city residents undergirds the utility of their identities. Nonetheless, it was useful to Larry and other church volunteers.

This examination of Downtown Church, then, has revealed three ideas to be useful in understanding the intersection of race, gender, class, the city, and its attendant congregational dynamics. A racialized urban imaginary formed the backdrop of thinking about what the city is and should be, and how a congregation that wants to be a church of and for the city should look and act. This imaginary shaped the congregation's goals, the images and marketing the staff used to promote it, and particular organizational practices that attempted to align the church with the imaginary. There were several dimensions to those practices. These included managed diversity, the set of principles that guided the pastoral leadership in trying to found and promote a diverse congregation, but one that was careful not to let particular forms of diversity dominate its self-presentation. Another was racial utility, the practice of displaying racial identities to achieve some desired congregational ends. During our observations, we found that both church leaders and congregants were informed by a consumption-oriented ideology and an assumption about a racialized authenticity that framed ideals for realizing religion in the city. Examining these cultural formations displayed how cultural values and religious identity are deeply embedded in the structures of race, especially when embodied in an urban location.

The Multiracial Urban Church Movement and Social Hopes

Religious organizations are one of the few social spaces where racial and ethnic minorities, in particular, can create their own social worlds and cultural worldviews free from the influences of dominant racial groups. In contrast to other social spaces where racial segregation has adversely affected outcomes for members of racial and ethnic minority groups, racial segregation in religious spaces continues to create a social space where these groups can thrive. In particular, the Black Church was historically an avenue of social mobility for African Americans, leading to education, secure employment, and status within the community and wider society. So why pursue a racially diverse religious congregation?

Multiracial urban congregations can matter for the greater society as congregants are seeking out spaces and ways to experience diversity and to have meaningful, cross-racial interactions in a deeply segregated society. Multiracial urban congregations remind us of the importance of studying the process by which actors in specific contexts reproduce or change social structures through their interactions—in this case, racial inclusion.

Racially diverse neighborhoods and metro areas across the nation are not immune to the legacy of racial residential segregation. Chicago's notorious racial residential segregation is one thing that shapes the drive of many of DC's congregants to pursue integration; these types of motivations make multiracial churches a vehicle for voluntary interaction with people from others races. Though the interactions are not perfect and often fraught with power struggles, they are still pursued in part due to the unlikelihood of integration in other parts of people's everyday lives (e.g., school, neighborhoods, or work settings). Downtown Church members' similar stage in the life cycle, such as being single, being early career, and not having children, provides some similar perspectives on life challenges and hopes. Perhaps these can trump other racial, class, and gender barriers that face member interactions at Down-town Church. But structural issues shape even the most willing interactions. Within the reproduction of racial inequality, there are classed and gendered interactions that remain the gatekeepers of what is feasible to achieve by way of inclusion. And yet, many members remain committed to the congregation, even through the management of diversity, and even through the occasionally obvious use of members' black identities and bodies for show without attendant organizational authority. This commitment even extends to a number of members whose pursuit of inclusion is manifest in an interracial romantic relationship, and who feel that they must hide that fact from the pastoral leadership. Leaders and church members are actively wrestling with race, and sometimes with each other, in complicated ways in their deliberate pursuits of the ideal urban church.

Interestingly, members of the congregation often express a desire for a "race-less" space to worship. As diversity is an assumed feature of the city landscape, many members initially are relieved by the lack of "race talk," and may well assume, or hope, that racial matters will take care of themselves. However, over time some of these members and others have come to interpret actions by leaders as showing a sort of ambivalence toward racial inclusion. Racial diversity is essential to the urban experience, an expected component of city churches. Cultural elements, like symbols of diversity, can contain many subjective and ambiguous interpretations. Congregants and staff may rely on the same symbol or trope without necessarily agreeing upon what it signifies. Some hold assumptions reflecting expectations that diversity is an egalitarian endeavor in which representation is equal throughout the organization, rather than something to experience or manipulate. Here members are expecting "self-consciously diverse communities" (Nyden et al. 1997) in which equal representation is institutionalized, rather than a community managed by a fairly closed circle of leadership.

This begs the question, *what is happening to the language of race?* The languages members and staff are using are different in assumption and implication, but they are talking about issues that involve considerations of oppression and inclusion. Downtown Church attendees and leaders are not using the "diversity buzz words" we have become accustomed to, but are still wrestling with issues that more self-conscious congregations, using more deliberative practices, have already worked through. Members and leaders of DC are bringing to light different constructions of racial interests and different racial thresholds for diversity within the congregation. These differences are in direct relationship to their interpretation of race matters in the city. Thus, place facilitates a different type of race work, and it appears to be associated with its own particular languages of inclusion.

While this book has focused on the complex relationship between spatial and religious identity, it has more broadly targeted the importance that organizational and local contexts have to the practices and accomplishment of inclusion. It would be instructive in furthering our understandings of place and organization to consider the superficial adaptations of diversity and inclusion occurring in other evangelical organizations across the country. Focusing on these types of urban congregations can offer us new ways to consider the continuous process of race-making and the negotiations of race in the twenty-first century. Localized racial formation in urban religious markets addresses the ways in which race travels across place. These emerging racial negotiations are informed by the unique racial histories embedded within these cities across the country, even as some patterns and cultural understandings transcend the local. While there is no reason to assume that multiracial congregational dynamics are the same in Atlanta, or San Diego, as they are in Chicago, overlap and similarities would be revealing. In this era of heightened mobility, it is an open question as to how different regional expressions of religion remain (but see Silk and Walsh 2008) as populations move. And at various points in American history, racial issues have been of prominent national importance, not to mention the breadth of federal law. Nonetheless, these dynamics are actually enacted at the local level, and that may assume varying forms.

As we situate the findings of this research within broader socio-religious debates about multiracial congregations, race, and religion, we argue for a more focused examination of congregations in urban settings. These congregations reveal more nuances in practices that are prescribed by differing visions of congregational diversity, ultimately speaking to the widely debated legacy and utility of the Evangelical Racial Change Movement. The intricacies and contradictions surrounding racially integrated congregations must be examined across intersections of spatial context, gender, and class as the next avenue for addressing race and religion. And while we know much about evangelical congregations, we know considerably less about how urban evangelical congregations matter for greater society. Similarly, we know less about other religious traditions, which may be significant as American cities become increasingly diverse with immigrants from around the world. Subsequently, if evangelical congregations continue with a pattern of seeking out church placements and memberships in downtown areas, how they interact with racially diverse environments will be a prism through which social scientists can explore the use of diversity tropes in pursuit of competing ends. This is particularly true in an era of rapidly changing racial landscapes and contemporary diversity agendas. Multiracial congregations in urban areas are a growing organizational trend among evangelicals, providing another avenue to explore three key cornerstones within American life: race, religion, and the city.

Place and the Making of Religion and Identity

Thinking about "place" sociologically is in many ways inherently intersectional. The idea has both social and geographical implications—we talk about "social locations" as sets of relationships among social statuses and social roles, and we talk about physical locations in which actual bodies reside. Both influence social attitudes, social behaviors, and social identities. And, as we have seen at Downtown Church, social and physical places come together to influence the relationships among race, religion, and gender. Urban spaces have a deep social and cultural connection to racial diversity, and this has religious dimensions. Part of religion is place (Williams 2005); it is where one belongs and is deeply implicated in the relationship between the divine and human societies. This varies by religious traditions, of course, with some more connected to particular sites than others. But sacred places are literal physical locations, whether built environments such as Mecca, the Vatican, and Jerusalem, or parts of the natural world such as the Ganges, Fujiyama, or Shiprock Mountain. The veneration of place is part of what makes a religion what it is and the denigration of a sacred place is experienced as a social and religious loss—even an assault—by the faithful. A religious place is where one—and one's god—"belongs."

Ethnicity and race are also placed. There are places where people of any particular type "belong." This can be a territory or nation or even a continent—which is part of what defines an ethnicity or race; people are "Italian" or "Midwestern" or "African American." "Go back to where you came from" is a frequent epithet hurled at immigrants, with the clear meaning that they don't belong here, they are out of place. The association in American thinking of "urban" with black, and with "small-town" America as white is part of this dynamic. Those things are basically true in the contemporary United States, in that African Americans disproportionately live in cities while small towns, especially in the Midwest and Great Plains regions, are overwhelmingly white. But they were not always true (before 1920 almost 90% of African Americans lived in rural areas) and our cultural imaginaries see them as "natural," as where people truly belong. Thus, often without thinking very carefully about it, we understand race and place to have a sacred quality—people of different races are where they belong and that belonging is similar to the belonging that comes from the connections between religion and place (Williams 2011, 2013).

Gender is also placed, in both the social and physical senses of the term. When someone claims that a "woman's place is in the home," they are using both meanings simultaneously. The home, taking care of family and especially children, is a social role but also a location that is out of the so-called public realms of the economy, politics, and the like. It is well established that many religious traditions validate and even sacralize this conception of gender appropriateness. Some faiths practice a strict gender segregation, keeping men and women in different literal places. Others, though not that strict, still see differences in the social and physical spaces appropriate for different genders. Even Downtown Church, which attracted many single, professional women, subordinated women's public leadership in the worship service and in church authority to men—particularly husbands. The idea behind DC's ill-advised "find a hot wife" episode continued the assumption that men were the core of the church and that women were, in the end, wives. That many people reacted to this episode negatively, and that many in the congregation would deny or dismiss any deliberate or explicit desire to keep women "in their place," doesn't change the fact that the unspoken and continuing assumptions that "place" gender nonetheless emerged.

Downtown Church is a specific religious congregation in a specific place. It has members, relationships, a history, and organizational challenges that are particularly its own. Nonetheless, an immersion into the ways in which a racialized urban imaginary shaped the congregation, and led to practices such as managed diversity and racial utility, has enriched our understanding of the ways in which space and cultural ideas about place are deeply entwined with racialized and gendered relationships. That these relationships happened in this case within a religious context is all the more illuminating—it opens a door for us to dig more deeply into the particularly American and the generally social ways that religion, race, and the city interact.

NOTES

INTRODUCTION
1. Portion of the Downtown Church mission statement.
2. We think it is not a coincidence that so much of this activity, such as Dwight Moody's famous church and Bible Institute, and Jane Addams's Hull House, and even James Lewis's history of Protestant efforts in Gary, Indiana, are centered on Chicago. We discuss Chicago, as a specific city, more fully in chapter 2.
3. All field notes and reports on interviews in this book reflect Barron's interactions in the field. Thus, all use of the first-person singular indicates Barron. The first-person plural is used whenever passages reflect our joint response to, and analysis of, the field notes, interview transcripts, and Downtown Church marketing materials.

CHAPTER 1. CITY JESUS
1. According to the 2007 American Community Survey distributed by the U.S. Census Bureau, Chicago is ranked as the fifteenth youngest city in North America. The 2010 US Census showed Chicago with a median age of 32. This is indeed younger than New York City (36), Los Angeles (34), Miami (40), Seattle (35), and San Francisco (37). But it is on par with, or older than, Orlando (32), St. Paul, Minnesota (32), Dallas (32), Houston (32), Salt Lake City (31), or Boston (31).
2. All pastors interviewed for this study were asked to provide data on the racial profile of the church and their responses were averaged. This approach is not uncommon when collecting demographic data on congregations. Nonetheless, the numbers presented here are approximate estimates and include international members. It also leaves open some ambiguity as to who fully counts as a "member." Many international congregants were students only visiting for three to six months, and most were from Europe, South America, and Australia.

CHAPTER 5. "SWIRL BABIES"
1. Upon completion of the fieldwork, Barron remained in contact with members of the group. As this manuscript was being developed, she received permission to include this story.

REFERENCES

Ammerman, Nancy Tatom. 1987. *Bible Believers: Fundamentalists in the Modern World*. New Brunswick, NJ: Rutgers University Press.

———. 1997. *Congregations and Community*. New Brunswick, NJ: Rutgers University Press.

———. 2005. *Pillars of Faith: American Congregations and Their Partners*. Berkeley: University of California Press.

Anderson, Benedict. 1991. *Imagined Communities: Reflections on the Origin and Spread of Nationalism*. New York: Verso.

Avishai, Orit. 2008. "'Doing Religion' in a Secular World: Women in Conservative Religions and the Question of Agency." *Gender & Society* 22: 409–433.

Badger, Emily, Quoctrung Bui, and Adam Pearce. 2016. "The Election Highlighted a Growing Rural-Urban Split." *New York Times*, November 11. www.nytimes.com.

Becker, Howard S. 1982. *Art Worlds*. Berkeley: University of California Press.

Becker, Penny Edgell. 1998. "Making Inclusive Communities: Congregations and the "Problem" of Race." *Social Problems* 45:451–472.

———. 1999. *Congregations in Conflict: Cultural Models of Local Religious Life*. Cambridge: Cambridge University Press.

Bell, Joyce M. and Douglas Hartmann. 2007. "Diversity in Everyday Discourse: The Cultural Ambiguities and Consequences of 'Happy Talk.'" *American Sociological Review* 72:895–914.

Bell, Michael M. 1995. *Childerley: Nature and Morality in a Country Village*. Chicago: University of Chicago Press.

Beltran, Mary and Camilla Fojas. 2008. *Mixed Race Hollywood*. New York: NYU Press.

Bennett, Larry. 2010. *The Third City: Chicago and American Urbanism*. Chicago: University of Chicago Press.

Berrey, Ellen. 2005. "Divided over Diversity: Political Discourse in a Chicago Neighborhood." *City and Community* 4:143–170.

———. 2011. "Why Diversity Became Orthodox in Higher Education, and How It Changed the Meaning of Race on Campus." *Critical Sociology* 35:573–596.

Blau, Peter. 1977. "A Macrosociological Theory of Social Structure." *American Journal of Sociology* 83(1).

Boehm, Lisa Krissoff. 2004. *Popular Culture and the Enduring Myth of Chicago, 1871–1968*. New York: Routledge.

Bonilla-Silva, Eduardo. 1997. "Rethinking Racism: Toward a Structural Analysis." *American Sociological Review* 62:465–480.

———. 2006. *Racism without Racists: Color-Blind Racism and the Persistence of Racial Inequality in the United States*, 2nd ed. Lanham, MD: Rowman & Littlefield.

Brown-Saracino, Japonica, Gary A. Fine, and Jessica Thurk. 2008. "Beyond Groups: Seven Pillars of Peopled Ethnography in Organizations and Communities." *Qualitative Research* 8:547–567.

Burawoy, Michael. 1998. "The Extended Case Method." *Sociological Theory* 16:4–33.

Chaves, Mark. 2004. *Congregations in America*. Cambridge, MA: Harvard University Press.

Chaves, Mark and Lynn M. Higgins. 1992. "Comparing the Community Involvement of Black and White Congregations." *Journal for the Scientific Study of Religion* 31:425–40.

Childs, Erica Chito. 2002. "Families on the Color-Line: Patrolling Borders and Crossing Boundaries." *Race and Society* 5:139–161.

———. 2008. "Listening to the Interracial Canary: Contemporary Views on Interracial Relationships Among Blacks and Whites." *Fordham Law Review* 76:2771–2786.

———. 2009. *Fade to Black and White*. Lanham, MD: Rowman & Littlefield.

Christerson, Brad, Korie L. Edwards, and Michael O. Emerson. 2005. *Against All Odds: The Struggle for Racial Integration in Religious Organizations*. New York: New York University Press.

Christerson, Brad, Korie L. Edwards, and Richard Flory. 2010. *Growing Up in America: The Power of Race in the Lives of Teens*. Stanford, CA: Stanford University Press.

Christerson, Brad and Michael O. Emerson 2003. "The Cost of Diversity in Religious Organizations: An In-Depth Case Study." *Sociology of Religion* 64:163–181.

Cobb, Ryon J., Samuel L. Perry, and Kevin D. Dougherty. 2015. "United by Faith? Race/Ethnicity, Congregational Diversity, and Explanations of Racial Inequality." *Sociology of Religion* 72 (2): 177–198.

Collins, Patricia Hill. 1999. *Black Feminist Thought: Knowledge, Consciousness, and the Politics of Empowerment*. New York: Routledge.

Collins, Sharon M. 1997. *Black Corporate Executives: The Making and Breaking of a Black Middle Class*. Philadelphia: Temple University Press.

———. 2011. "From Affirmative Action to Diversity: Erasing Inequality from Organizational Responsibility." *Critical Sociology* 37:517.

Crenshaw, Kimberle. 1993. "Mapping the Margins: Intersectionality, Identity Politics and Violence Against Women of Color." *Stanford Law Review* 43(6): 1241–1299.

Delgado, Richard and Stefancic, Jean, eds. 1995. *Critical Race Theory: The Cutting Edge*. Philadelphia: Temple University Press.

DeYoung, Curtiss Paul, Michael O. Emerson, George Yancey, and Karen Chai Kim. 2003. *United by Faith: the Multiracial Congregation as an Answer to the Problem of Race*. New York: Oxford University Press.

Dougherty, Kevin D. and Kimberly R. Huyser. 2008. "Racially Diverse Congregations: Organizational Identity and the Accommodation of Differences." *Journal for the Scientific Study of Religion* 47:23–43.

Dougherty, Kevin D. and Mark T. Mulder. 2009. "Congregational Responses to Growing Ethnic Diversity in a White Ethnic Denomination." *Social Problems* 56:335–356.

Drake, St. Claire and Horace R. Cayton. 1970/1945. *Black Metropolis: A Study of Negro Life in a Northern City*. Revised and Enlarged Edition. New York: Harcourt, Brace & World.

Duncan, James S. and Nancy G. Duncan. 2004. *Landscapes of Privilege: The Politics of the Aesthetic in an American Suburb*. New York: Routledge.

Durr, Marlese and Adina M. Harvey Wingfield. 2011. "Keeping your 'N' in Check: African American Women and the Interactive Effects of Etiquette and Emotional Labor." *Critical Sociology* 37:557–571.

Edwards, Korie L. 2008. *The Elusive Dream: The Power or Race in Interracial Churches*. New York: Oxford University Press.

Edwards, Korie L., Brad Christerson, and Michael O. Emerson. 2013. "Race, Religious Organizations, and Integration." *Annual Review of Sociology* 39:211–228.

Ellingson, Stephen. 2007. *The Megachurch and the Mainline: Remaking Religious Tradition in the Twenty-first Century*. Chicago: University of Chicago Press.

Emerson, Michael O., Korie L. Edwards, Gerardo Marti, and Kathleen Garces-Foley. 2008. "Forum on Racially and Ethnically Diverse Congregations." *Journal for the Scientific Study of Religion* 47 (1): 1–22.

Emerson, Michael O. and Christian Smith. 2000. *Divided by Faith: Evangelical Religion and the Problem of Race in America*. New York: Oxford University Press.

Emerson, Michael O. and Rodney Woo. 2006. *People of the Dream: Multiracial Congregations in the United States*. Princeton, NJ: Princeton University Press.

Emerson, Michael O. and George Yancey. 2008. "African Americans in Interracial Congregations: An Analysis of Demographics, Social Networks, and Social Attitudes." *Review of Religious Research* 49:301–318.

Feldman, Martha S., Jeannine Bell, and Michele Tracy Berger. 2003. *Gaining Access*. Walnut Creek, CA: Altamira Press.

Finke, Roger and Rodney Stark. 1992. *The Churching of America, 1776–1990: Winners and Losers in Our Religious Economy*. New Brunswick, NJ: Rutgers University Press.

Flory, Richard and Donald E. Miller. 2008. *Finding Faith: The Spiritual Quest of the Post-Boomer Generation*. New Brunswick, NJ: Rutgers University Press.

Form, William and Joshua Dubrow. 2005. "Downtown Metropolitan Churches: Ecological Situation and Response." *Journal for the Scientific Study of Religion* 44: 271–290.

Frankenberg, Ruth. 1993. *White Women, Race Matters: The Social Construction of Whiteness*. Minneapolis: University of Minnesota Press.

Gamio, Lazaro. 2016. "Urban and Rural America Are Becoming Increasingly Polarized: Since Obama's Election in 2008, The Trend of Urban Counties Voting for Democrats and Rural Counties Voting for Republicans Has Grown Stronger." *Washington Post*, November 17, 2016. www.washingtonpost.com.

Grazian, David. 2004. *Blue Chicago: The Search for Authenticity in Urban Blues Clubs*. Chicago: University of Chicago Press.

———. 2007. *On the Make: The Hustle of Urban Nightlife.* Chicago: University of Chicago Press.

Greenberg, Miriam. 2008. *Branding New York: How a City in Crisis Was Sold to the World.* New York: Routledge.

Gusfield, Joseph R. 1963. *Symbolic Crusade: Status Politics and the American Temperance Movement.* Urbana: University of Illinois Press.

Hammond, Phillip E. 1992. *Religion and Personal Autonomy: The Third Disestablishment in America.* Columbia: University of South Carolina Press.

Higham, John. 1955. *Strangers in the Land: Patterns of American Nativism, 1860–1925.* New Brunswick, NJ: Rutgers University Press.

Hoelscher, Steven. 2003. "Making Place, Making Race: Performances of Whiteness in the Jim Crow South." *Annals of the Association of American Geographers* 93 (3): 657–686.

Holland, Megan M. 2012. "Only Here for the Day: The Social Integration of Minority Students at a Majority White High School." *Sociology of Education* 85:101–119.

hooks, bell. 1993. *Black Looks: Race and Representation.* Boston: South End Press.

Hummon, David M. 1990. *Commonplaces: Community Ideology and Identity in American Culture.* Albany: State University of New York Press.

Hunt, Larry L. and Matthew O. Hunt. 2001. "Race, Religion, and Religious Involvement: A Comparison of White and African Americans Church Attendance." *Social Forces* 80:605–631.

Irby, Courtney Ann. 2013. "We Didn't Call It Dating: The Disrupted Landscape of Relationship Advice for Evangelical Protestant Youth." *Critical Research on Religion* 2:177–194.

———. 2014. "Moving Beyond Agency: A Review of Gender and Intimate Relationships in Conservative Religions." *Sociological Compass* pp. 1269–1280.

Johnson, Patrick. 2003. *Appropriating Blackness: Performance and the Politics of Authenticity.* Durham, NC: Duke University Press.

Jorstad, Erling. 1993. *Popular Religion in America: The Evangelical Voice.* Westport, CT: Greenwood Press.

Lee, Barrett, John Iceland, and Gregory Sharp. 2012. *Racial and Ethnic Diversity Goes Local: Charting Change in American Communities Over Three Decades.* US2010 Project, Department of Sociology and Population Research Institute: The Pennsylvania State University.

Lee, Jennifer and Frank D. Bean. 2007. "Reinventing the Color Line: Immigration and America's New Racial/Ethnic Divide." *Social Forces* 86:561–586.

Lewis, James W. 1992. *The Protestant Experience in Gary, Indiana, 1906–1975: At Home in the City.* Knoxville: University of Tennessee Press.

Lichterman, Paul, Prudence L. Carter, and Michele Lamont. 2009. "Race-Bridging for Christ? Conservative Christians and Black-White Relations in Community Life." Pp. 187–220 in *Evangelicals and Democracy in America*, edited by Steven Brint and Jean Reith Schroedel. New York: Russell Sage Foundation.

Lincoln, C. Eric and Lawrence H. Mamiya. 1990. *The Black Church in the African American Experience.* Durham, NC: Duke University Press.

Lloyd, Richard. 2006. *Neo-Bohemia: Art and Commerce in the Postindustrial City.* New York: Routledge.

Lorde, Audre. 1984. *Sister Outsider: Essays and Speeches.* New York: Crossing Press.

Luker, Ralph E. 1998. *The Social Gospel in Black and White: American Racial Reform, 1885–1912.* Chapel Hill: University of North Carolina Press.

Marti, Gerardo. 2005. *A Mosaic of Believers: Diversity and Innovation in a Multiethnic Church.* Bloomington: Indiana University Press.

———. 2008. *Hollywood Faith: Holiness, Prosperity, and Ambition in a Los Angeles Church.* New Brunswick, NJ: Rutgers University Press.

———. 2009. "Affinity, Identity, and Transcendence: The Experience of Religious Racial Integration in Diverse Congregations." *Journal for the Scientific Study of Religion* 48:53– 68.

———. 2012. *Worship Across the Racial Divide: Religious Music and the Multiracial Congregation.* New York: Oxford University Press.

Marti, Gerardo and Michael O. Emerson. 2014. "The Rise of the Diversity Expert: How American Evangelicals Simultaneously Accentuate and Ignore Race." Pp. 179–199 in *The New Evangelical Social Engagement*, edited by Brian Steensland and Philip Goff. New York: Oxford University Press.

Marti, Gerardo and Gladys Ganiel. 2014. *The Deconstructed Church: Understanding Emerging Christianity.* New York: Oxford University Press.

Martinez, Brandon C. and Kevin D. Dougherty. 2013. "Race, Belonging, and Participation in Religious Congregations." *Journal for the Scientific Study of Religion* 52:713–732.

Marvasti, Amir B. and Karyn D. McKinney. 2011. "Does Diversity Mean Assimilation?" *Critical Sociology* 37:631–650.

Massey, Douglas S. and Nancy A. Denton. 1993. *American Apartheid.* Cambridge, MA: Harvard University Press.

McClintock, Elizabeth Aura. 2010. "When Does Race Matter? Race, Sex, and Dating at an Elite University." *Journal of Marriage and Family* 72:45–71.

McLoughlin, William G. 1980. *Revivals, Awakenings, and Reform.* Chicago: University of Chicago Press.

McRoberts, Omar. 2003. *Streets of Glory: Church and Community in a Black Urban Neighborhood.* Chicago: University of Chicago Press.

Mele, Christopher. 2000. *Selling the Lower East Side: Culture, Real Estate, and Resistance in New York City.* Minneapolis: University of Minnesota Press.

Molotch, Harvey L. 1972. *Managed Integration: Dilemmas of Doing Good in the City.* Berkeley: University of California Press.

Moon, Dawne. 2013. "Powerful Emotions: Symbolic Power and the (Productive and Punitive) Force of Collective Feeling." *Theory and Society* 42:261–294.

Nyden, Philip, Anne Figert, Mark Shibley, and Darryl Burrows. 1997. *Building Community: Social Science in Action.* Thousand Oaks, CA: Pine Forge Press.

Olson, Daniel V. A. 1989. "Church Friendships: Boon or Barrier to Church Growth." *Journal for Scientific Study of Religion* 28:432–447.

———. 2008. "Why Do Small Religious Groups Have More Committed Members?" *Review of Religious Research* 49:353–378.

Omi, Michael and Howard Winant. 1994. *Racial Formation in the United States: From 1960s to 1990s*. New York: Routledge.

Orsi, Robert A. 1999. *Gods of the City*. Bloomington: Indiana University Press.

Pattillo-McCoy, Mary. 1999. *Black Picket Fences: Privilege and Peril Among the Black Middle Class*. Chicago: University of Chicago Press.

———. 2007. *Black on the Block: The Politics of Race and Class in the City*. Chicago: University of Chicago Press.

Perry, Samuel L. 2013. "Religion and Interracial Romance: The Effects of Religious Affiliation, Public Devotional Practices, and Biblical Literalism." *Social Science Quarterly* 94(5): 1308–1327.

Peterson, Richard A. 1997. *Creating Country Music: Fabricating Authenticity*. Chicago: University of Chicago Press.

Price, Matthew. 2000. "Place, Race, and History: The Social Mission of Downtown Churches." Pp. 57–82 in *Public Religion and Urban Transformation: Faith in the City*, edited by Lowell W. Livezey. New York: New York University Press.

Read, Jen'nan and David E. Eagle. 2011. "Intersecting Identities as a Source of Religious Incongruence." *Journal for the Scientific Study of Religion* 50:116–132.

Reed, Christopher Robert. 2011. *The Rise of Chicago's Black Metropolis, 1920–1929*. Urbana: University of Illinois Press.

Rockquemore, Kerry Ann and Brunsma, David. 2001. *Beyond Black: Biracial Identity in America*. Thousand Oaks, CA: Sage.

Rodriquez, Jason. 2006. "Color-blind Ideology and the Cultural Appropriation of Hip-hop." *Journal of Contemporary Ethnography* 35:645–668.

Roof, Wade Clark. 1999. *Spiritual Marketplace: Baby Boomers and the Remaking of American Religion*. Princeton, NJ: Princeton University Press.

Royster, Deirdre A. 2003. *Race and the Invisible Hand: How White Networks Exclude Black Men From Blue-Collar Jobs*. Berkeley: University of California Press.

Russell-Brown, Katheryn. 2008. *The Color of Crime: Racial Hoaxes, White Fear, Black Protectionism, Police Harassment, and Other Macroaggressions*. 2nd ed. New York: New York University Press.

Sampson, Robert J. 2013. *Great American City: Chicago and the Enduring Neighborhood Effect*. Chicago: University of Chicago Press.

Schrag, Peter. 2010. *Not Fit for Our Society: Immigration and Nativism in America*. Berkeley: University of California Press.

Silk, Mark and Andrew Walsh. 2008. *One Nation, Divisible: How Regional Religious Differences Shape American Politics*. Lanham, MD: Rowman & Littlefield Publishers.

Thumma, Scott and Dave Travis. 2007. *Beyond Megachurch Myths: What We Can Learn from America's Largest Churches*. San Francisco: Jossey-Bass.

Wacquant, Loïc. 2001. "Deadly Symbiosis: When Ghetto and Prison Meet and Mesh." *Punishment & Society* 3:95–134.

Wacquant, Loïc and William Julius Wilson. 1997. "The Cost of Racial and Class Exclusion in the Inner City." Pp. 341–353 in *The Urban Sociology Reader*, edited by Richard T. LeGates and Frederic Stout. New York: Routledge Press.

Wadsworth, Nancy D. 2014. *Ambivalent Miracles: Evangelicals and the Politics of Racial Healing.* Charlottesville: University of Virginia Press.

Warner, R. Stephen. 1990. *New Wine in Old Wineskins: Evangelicals and Liberals in a Small Town Church.* Berkeley: University of California Press.

Warner, Stephen and J. G. Wittner, eds. 1998. *Gatherings in Diaspora: Religious Communities and the New Immigration.* Philadelphia: Temple University Press.

Wellman, James K. 1999. *The Gold Coast Church and the Ghetto: Christ and Culture in Mainline Protestantism.* Urbana: University of Illinois Press.

Whyte, William. Foote. 1993. *Street Corner Society: The Social Structure of an Italian Slum.* Chicago: University of Chicago Press.

Wilkens Amy C. 2008. "'Happier than non-Christians': Collective Emotions and Symbolic Boundaries among Evangelical Christians." *Social Psychology Quarterly* 71:281–301.

Williams, Rhys H. 2002. "Religion, Community, and Place: Locating the Transcendent." Review Essay. *Religion and American Culture: A Journal of Interpretation* 12, no. 2 (Summer): 249–263.

———. 2004. "Religion and Place in the Midwest: Urban, Rural, and Suburban Forms of Religious Expression." Pp. 187–208 in *Religion and Public Life in the Midwest: America's Common Denominator*, edited by Philip Barlow and Mark Silk. Walnut Creek, CA: Altamira Press.

———2005. "Introduction to a Forum on Religion and Place." *Journal for the Scientific Study of Religion* 44 (3):239–242.

———. 2006. "Religion in the City: Confronting the 'Other' Every Day." Pp. 21–38 in *Varieties of Urban Experience: The American City and the Practice of Culture*, edited by Michael Ian Borer. Lanham, MD: University Press of America.

———. 2011. "Creating an American Islam: Thoughts on Religion, Identity, and Place." *Sociology of Religion* 72 (2):127–153.

———. 2013. "Civil Religion and the Cultural Politics of National Identity in Obama's America." *Journal for the Scientific Study of Religion* 52 (2):239–257.

———. 2015. "Religion and Multiculturalism: A Web of Legal, Institutional, and Cultural Connections." *Sociological Quarterly* 56 (4):607–622.

———. 2016. "Religion and Immigration Post-1965: Race, Culture Wars, and National Identity." Pp. 278–290 in *The Wiley-Blackwell Companion to Religion & Politics in the U.S.*, edited by Barbara A. McGraw. Malden, MA: Wiley-Blackwell.

Williams, Rhys H., Courtney Ann Irby, and R. Stephen Warner. 2016. "'Church' in Black and White: The Organizational Lives of Young Adults." *Religions* 7:90.

Wilson, William Julius 1996. *When Work Disappears.* New York: Knopf.

Yancey, George and Ye Jung Kim. 2008. "Racial Diversity, Gender Equality, and SES Diversity in Christian Congregations: Exploring the Connections of Racism, Sexism, and Classism in Multiracial and Non-multiracial Churches." *Journal for the Scientific Study of Religion* 47:103–111.

Zukin, Sharon. 1993. *Landscapes of Power: From Detroit to Disney World.* Berkeley: University of California Press.

———. 1995. *The Cultures of Cities.* Oxford: Blackwell.

———. 2004. *Point of Purchase: How Shopping Changed American Culture.* New York: Routledge.

INDEX

Alcohol: in church advertising, 50–53; in rented church space, 51–53

Ammerman, Nancy Tatom, 12, 18

Ambivalence, 72, 130, 138–139, 175; and religious commitment, 157; and resistance, 141–143

Anderson, Benedict, 13

Authenticity, 13, 19, 29, 46, 47, 52, 65, 69, 72, 120, 164, 169–170, 171; and Chicago identity, 33–34; as fabricated, 14–15; and physical appearance, 155; and place, 15, 30; "racialized," 21, 105, 174; and religious commitment, 158; stereotypes of, 31; and urban black culture, 75, 96, 168; as urban church, 29–30, 120, 166; in worship services, 147

Authority, 20; members' resistance to, 109, 120, 172; organizational, 10, 32–39, 68, 79, 96, 130, 139, 163, 171, 175; pastoral, 34, 37, 121; pastoral and dating relationships, 125, 127, 129–30, 132, 136, 138–141

Avishai, Orit, 156

Becker, Penny Edgell, 18, 89, 97

Bell, Joyce M., 76

Bonilla-Silva, Eduardo, 142

Branding, 8, 43, 48, 53, 65, 66, 167; through appearance and sexual allure, 55–58, 60–61, 67; through church advertising, 25, 48–50, 53–54; and the home church, 24; and member education, 114; through outreach ministries, 103–104, 115–116; and technology, 63

Brunsma, David, 140

Capital: color, 120; cultural, 67, 95, 114, 118, 119; symbolic, 96, 111, 118, 120

Cayton, Horace, 41

Chaves, Mark, 9, 18, 166

Chicago, 20, 26, 28–29, 41–42, 51, 170, 181; association with African Americans, 29, 41–42, 73, 168–170; and authenticity, 33–34, 167–168; and "Chicagoland," 32–33, 34–35; and church business, 116, 118–119; and fashion, 35–36; as needing the church, 152–154; and racial segregation 46, 63, 153–154, 174; as "unchurched," 28–29, 153, 167; as "young" city, 28. *See also* City; Racialized urban imaginary

Christerson, Brad, 160

City: and cultural excitement, 4, 13, 27, 36; as cultural idea, 5–8, 165, 167–168; and diversity, 5; and immigration, 5–6; racial percentages of residents, 11–12, 169; and sexuality, 60; versus the suburbs, 34, 37. *See also* Racialized urban imaginary

Class, 4, 7; and congregational leadership, 31, 39, 64–65, 106; and middle-class consumption, 30, 47, 50–55, 62–64, 67, 70, 163; and "nocturnal experience," 50, 55, 68; and outreach ministries, 112, 114; and physical appearance, 57–59; and racial commodification, 42–43; and target members, 25, 27, 42, 54; and technology, 62–63; and urban imaginary, 15, 21, 46, 63

Colorblind ideology, 95, 119, 125, 129; in pastoral staff's outlook, 89, 126; in personal relationships, 126, 127, 129, 140–141

ABOUT THE AUTHORS

Jessica M. Barron (PhD, Texas A&M University) is a Consultant and Researcher at Frontline Solutions in Durham, North Carolina. Her research interest focuses on the intersection of race/ethnicity and racial segregation on attitudes and identities in the United States. Her publications include *Managed Diversity: Race, Place, and an Urban Church* (2016), which won the Association for the Sociology of Religion's 2017 Distinguished Article Award, and *Structures of Privilege and Oppression: Multiracial Americans and the U.S. Racial Hierarchy* (with M. Campbell 2014).

Rhys H. Williams (PhD, University of Massachusetts, Amherst) is Professor of Sociology and Director of the McNamara Center for the Social Study of Religion at Loyola University Chicago. His publications include *Religion & Progressive Activism* (New York University Press 2017, with T. N. Fuist and R. Braunstein), *Promise Keepers and the New Masculinity* (2001), *Cultural Wars in American Politics* (1997), and articles in the *American Sociological Review, Social Problems, Sociological Theory, Theory & Society,* and the *Journal for the Scientific Study of Religion.*